The United Nations

Also by I. G. Edmonds

THE KHMERS OF CAMBODIA: *The Story of a Mysterious People*
TAIWAN: *The Other China*
THAILAND: *The Golden Land*
THE NEW MALAYSIA

THE UNITED NATIONS

Successes
and
Failures

by I. G. Edmonds

THE BOBBS-MERRILL COMPANY, INC.

INDIANAPOLIS / NEW YORK

To Annette

ISBN 0–672–51749–3
Library of Congress catalog card number 73–13229
Designed by Jack Jaget
Manufactured in the United States of America

First printing

Contents

Introduction

In the spring of 1945, as one of the most devastating wars in history was drawing to a close, representatives of war-weary nations met in San Francisco, California, to try to find a way to end war forever. Their answer to the challenge of permanent peace was the formation of the United Nations, an organization where civilized debate would take the place of slaughter on the battlefield.

More than a quarter of a century has passed since the original fifty-one nations signed the Charter for the United Nations, pledging themselves to use peaceful means for solving international disputes. During this time there has not been a single day that war in some form has not been fought somewhere in the world. In fact, it is doubtful if any period in history has seen such widespread international unrest. India and Pakistan have fought two wars. The Israelis and the Arabs have been involved in continual disputes. Indonesia fought a war for independence with the Netherlands and then made aggressive attacks on Malaysia. Malaysia fought a twelve-year war with Communist guerrillas. Russia crushed Hungary and then intervened in Czechoslovakia with bloody results. The United States led the UN into war in Korea, then became bogged down in Vietnam in the longest war in American history.

There was also trouble in Jordan, Iran, Lebanon, Greece, Malta, Burma, Suez, and Bangladesh, and in the Congo, where fighting produced the worst atrocities of modern times. In almost all of these events the United Nations, founded to keep world peace, failed to do so. At this point in UN history young people can well ask, "If the United Nations has failed as a peace keeper in the past, what hope can we place in it for the future?"

This is a question that anyone can—and should—ask with genuine concern, for hope of ending war in the future rests with the United Nations—a seeming failure. The question becomes even more pertinent to Americans because the United States has lost the leadership it exercised in the UN in the past. The balance of power in the world organization is shifting to nations in opposition to American objectives and ideals.

Many international observers believe that the United Nations must make some radical changes in its Charter if it ever hopes to become an effective agent for peace. Not all these critics are outsiders; many are members of various national delegations to the world body. One of them was no less a personage than Adam Malik of Indonesia, the 1971–72 president of the UN General Assembly.

However, no organization can be judged solely on its failures. The United Nations has also had its successes. In order to properly answer the question, "What can the UN do for us who must live in the world of tomorrow?" one must weigh the UN's successes against its failures. UN successes have not always been so spectacular as its failures and therefore have received less publicity. Millions of people probably never heard of most of them. Yet some of these seemingly minor successes may in time prove of great world value.

This is why people everywhere need to understand the UN better. Understanding can come only through a study of the UN's successes and failures and the reasons behind them. In this way we can hopefully get some idea of how the United Nations can help us in the years to come, and, even more important, how we can lend it our support in working toward a better world and a more peaceful tomorrow.

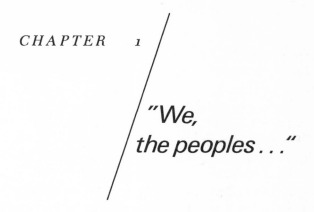

CHAPTER 1

*"We,
the peoples..."*

WE, THE PEOPLES OF THE UNITED NATIONS, determined to save succeeding generations from the scourge of war, which twice in our lifetime has brought untold sorrow to mankind, and

to reaffirm faith in fundamental human rights, in the dignity and worth of the human person, in the equal rights of men and women and of nations large and small, and

to establish conditions under which justice and respect for the obligations arising from treaties and other sources of international law can be maintained, and

to promote social progress and better standards of life in larger freedom

AND FOR THESE ENDS

to practice tolerance and live together in peace with one another as good neighbors, and to unite our strength to maintain international peace and security, and

to insure, by acceptance of principles and the institution of methods, that armed force shall not be used, save in the common interest, and

to employ international machinery for the promotion of the economic and social advancement of all peoples,

HAVE RESOLVED TO COMBINE OUR EFFORTS TO ACCOMPLISH THESE AIMS.

Accordingly, our respective Governments, through representatives assembled in the city of San Francisco, who have exhibited their full powers found to be in good and due form, have agreed to the present Charter of the United Nations and do hereby establish an international organization to be known as the United Nations.

In these words, drafted by Jan Christian Smuts, prime minister of the Union of South Africa, fifty nations declared their intention to find a workable way to bring peace to the world and dignity to mankind. Fifty-one nations had been invited to the 1945 San Francisco conference to form the United Nations. One, Poland, was having difficulty forming a government and did not send a delegation. However, Poland was permitted to sign the Charter of the United Nations later, bringing the number of original signers to fifty-one.

Smuts's resolution was adopted as the preamble to the Charter. The nineteen chapters and 111 articles that make up the Charter had largely been worked out in international conferences prior to the meeting. In the short time of two months, details were worked out, and the chief of each national delegation signed the Charter on behalf of his country.

The final article of the Charter read:

The present Charter, of which the Chinese, French, Russian, English and Spanish texts are equally authentic, shall remain deposited in the archives of the Government of the United States of America. Duly certified copies thereof shall be transmitted by that Government to the Governments of the other signatory States.

IN FAITH WHEREOF the representatives of the Governments of the United Nations have signed the present Charter.

DONE at the city of San Francisco the twenty-sixth day of June, one thousand nine hundred and forty-five.

China	Haiti
Union of Soviet	Honduras
Socialist Republics	India
United Kingdom	Iran
United States	Iraq
of America	Lebanon
France	Liberia
Argentina	Luxembourg
Australia	Mexico
Belgium	Netherlands
Bolivia	New Zealand
Brazil	Nicaragua
Byelorussian Soviet	Norway
Socialist Republic	Panama

Canada	Paraguay
Chile	Peru
Colombia	Philippine
Costa Rica	Commonwealth
Cuba	Poland
Czechoslovakia	Saudi Arabia
Denmark	Syria
Dominican Republic	Turkey
Ecuador	Ukrainian Soviet
Egypt	Socialist Republic
El Salvador	Union of South Africa
Ethiopia	Uruguay
Greece	Venezuela
Guatemala	Yugoslavia

After the delegates signed the Charter, it had to be ratified by the participating governments. This took another four months, and then the United Nations officially came into being on October 24, 1945—a date that is now celebrated as United Nations Day.

The concept of a world body dedicated to keeping the peace was hardly new when the United Nations Charter was adopted in San Francisco. The idea goes all the way back to Grecian times. One of those who foresaw not only its need but also its final form was William Penn, the founder of Pennsylvania. In 1693 Penn, in an "Essay Toward the Present and Future Peace of Europe," envisioned an international parliament modeled on the British House of Commons that could hear disputes when ordinary diplomacy failed. However, Penn's international parliament would have had the power to enforce its decisions. The United Nations does not have this power, except in a limited way.

Penn's idea did not impress the diplomats of his day,

and it was not until 1920 that the League of Nations was formed to do what Penn advocated in 1693. The League, unfortunately, also had no power to enforce its decisions. The United States refused to join the League. Russia joined late but was expelled for invading Finland without provocation. Japan, Italy, and Germany resigned in order to continue their individual aggressions in China, Ethiopia, and Czechoslovakia. This left the League so disorganized and ineffective that it could do absolutely nothing when Japan invaded Manchuria, or when Hitler moved into the Rhineland in opposition to World War I treaties, or when Italy attacked Ethiopia.

World War II broke out in September, 1939, and by early 1941 Hitler was in command of Europe and threatening to invade England. The United States was not yet in the war, but President Franklin D. Roosevelt realized that it was only a matter of time before this would happen. He was already violating all principles of neutrality in aiding the British and then went a step further in meeting with Prime Minister Winston Churchill on a ship in the Atlantic Ocean to "map a common program of purposes and principles." The result was a "Joint Declaration of the President of the United States and the Prime Minister of the United Kingdom." This declaration became known as the "Atlantic Charter." One of the principles laid down in the Atlantic Charter called for international cooperation in enforcing peace.

This portion of the Atlantic Charter is considered to be the seed from which the United Nations grew. The next step was the "Declaration by United Nations," which was signed in Washington, D.C., on January 1, 1942, just after the United States had entered the war. It was signed by all twenty-six nations then at war against Germany and Japan. Later an additional twenty-one nations signed the declaration. This was the first time the words "United Nations" had been used. The original draft of the Declaration had referred to the nations as the "Allies," but President Roosevelt suggested that the term Allies (which had been used in World War I) be replaced with the term "United Nations."

The "Declaration by United Nations" pledged the allied countries to support one another during the war and to support the Atlantic Charter with its call for international cooperation to enforce peace.

The next step in the development of the United Nations was the Moscow Declaration signed by the foreign ministers of China, the United Kingdom, the United States, and Soviet Russia in October, 1943. Here for the first time an agreement was reached to form a peace-keeping organization after the war. The U.S. State Department Bulletin of November 6, 1943, reported ". . . that they [the four nations signing the Moscow Declaration] recognize the necessity of establishing at the earliest practicable date a general international organization, based on the principle of the sovereign equality of all peace-loving States, and open to membership by all such States, large and small, for the maintenance of international peace and security."

After the Moscow Declaration, things moved swiftly. President Roosevelt was the strongest supporter of the future United Nations. He remembered very well that President Woodrow Wilson had likewise supported the League of Nations after World War I, but had been defeated by American isolationists in Congress in all his attempts to bring the United States into the League. Roosevelt feared that the same reaction would occur after World War II ended. Therefore he pushed hard to get the United Nations formed and make the United States a member while the war was still going on.

Seven months after the Moscow Declaration was signed, Roosevelt announced that a draft plan for a world peace-keeping organization had been completed by a team from the U.S. Department of State. He then invited China, Russia, and the United Kingdom (Great Britain) to a conference at Dumbarton Oaks, an estate in Washington, D.C., to consider the plan.

The plan was based on the old League of Nations. There would be an Assembly, but unlike the League the real power would be vested in a Security Council. Russia, China, the United States, and Great Britain reserved permanent places for themselves on the Security Council. The remaining seven seats would be filled by representatives of other nations who would be elected by the General Assembly for two-year periods. The conferees at Dumbarton Oaks agreed on all points except the voting procedure in the Security Council. The conference adjourned in October, 1944.

Then in February, 1945, the voting question was settled by Marshal Stalin of Russia, President Roosevelt, and Winston Churchill of the United Kingdom in a meeting at Yalta in the Crimea. They agreed that questions involving keeping the peace would be settled by a majority of seven votes from the eleven members of the Security Council, but that the vote must include the concurrence of all the permanent members. This gave Russia, China, the United Kingdom, and the United States the power to veto any peace proposal in the Security Council *simply by voting against it.* This decision was to have fateful results in the years to come.

Another difficult question that the Big Three had to settle was the allocation of votes in the General Assembly. Foreign Minister Molotov of Russia pointed out that each of the British Commonwealth nations would have a vote since Canada and Australia would be admitted as individual countries. This would give the United Kingdom the effect of having several votes in the Assembly. Molotov then demanded that the Soviet Union be given one vote for each of its individual soviet states.

Cordell Hull, the U.S. secretary of state, reported this demand to President Roosevelt before the American president was to meet with Stalin and Churchill to iron out final UN problems. Roosevelt, although near death at the time, still retained his jaunty confidence. He stuck his long cigarette holder in his mouth and replied, "If Stalin presses the point, then I'll ask for one vote in the Assembly for each of our forty-eight states!"

In the showdown Roosevelt and Stalin agreed to give Russia three votes by admitting the Ukrainian Soviet Socialist Republic and the Byelorussian Soviet Socialist Republic to membership as individual states. They also agreed that the United States could have three votes in the General Assembly as well. However, the concession to the United States caused such an outcry among smaller nations that the United States dropped this provision at the San Francisco conference, taking only a single vote.

Seven days after this summit conference, which ended February 11, 1945, the U.S. State Department made this announcement:

> For . . . eight days, Winston S. Churchill, Prime Minister of Great Britain, Franklin D. Roosevelt, president of the United States, and Marshal J. V. Stalin, Chairman of the Council of the People's Commissars of the Union of Soviet Socialist Republics, have met with the Foreign Secretaries, Chiefs of Staff, and other advisors in the Crimea. . . .
>
> It was decided:

1. That a United Nations Conference on the proposed World Organization should be summoned for Wednesday, April 25th, 1945, and should be held in the United States of America.

2. The nations to be invited to this conference should be:

(a) The United Nations as they existed on February 8th, 1945 [This meant those nations actually at war with the Axis powers on this date]: and

(b) Such of the Associated Nations as have declared war on the common enemy by March 1st, 1945. [This was to put pressure to declare war on those nations which were sympathetic to the Allied cause but which had not actually entered the war.] When the Conference on World Organization is held, the delegates of the United Kingdom and United States of America will support a proposal to admit to original membership two Soviet Socialist Republics, i.e., the Ukraine and White Russia [Byelorussia].

3. That the United States Government, on behalf of the Three Powers [that is, Russia, Great Britain, and the U.S.], should consult the Government of China and the French Provisional Government in regard to decisions taken at the present Conference concerning the proposed World Organization.

France had not been invited to the conference at Yalta, which infuriated General Charles De Gaulle who headed the French government in exile. Roosevelt, while agreeing that he did not want the temperamental De Gaulle at Yalta, had wanted to include Chiang Kai-shek of China. Stalin flatly refused. China was at war with Japan, and Russia had not yet entered the war against the Japanese. Stalin claimed that including China in the Yalta conference would be interpreted by Japan as an unfriendly act.

This was a rather curious reason for excluding Chiang Kai-shek from the Yalta conference, since the concluding paragraph of the joint statement signed on February 11, 1945, by Stalin, Roosevelt, and Churchill, said:

> For its part, the Soviet Union expresses its readiness to conclude with the National Government of China a pact of friendship and alliance between the U.S.S.R. and China in order to render assistance to China and its armed forces for the purpose of liberating China from the Japanese yoke.

This statement could hardly be interpreted by the Japanese as anything but unfriendly.

The agreements concerning the proposed United Nations ended with a statement that the United States would issue invitations for other nations to join in the San Francisco conference to consider a United Nations Charter based on the agreements reached at Dumbarton Oaks as modified by the Yalta conference.

The decision to hold the Charter conference in the United States was unanimous. Stalin did not want conferees coming into Russia, for he looked on them as spies, and he was extremely suspicious of Winston Churchill. This caused him to dislike the idea of the conference being held in England. Churchill, in turn, remembering how the old League of Nations had been rejected by the U.S. Senate, thought that holding the conference in the United States would help stir up support there for the United Nations.

Roosevelt was not destined to see the United Nations become a reality. He died two months and one day after the close of the Yalta conference. Harry S. Truman became president when Roosevelt died on Thursday, April

12, 1945. Fortunately for the United Nations, Truman staunchly supported the idea of a world peace-keeping body. In his first address to Congress after becoming president, Truman said, "Nothing is more essential to the future peace of the world than the continued cooperation of the nations which had to muster the force necessary to defeat the conspiracy of the Axis powers to dominate the world."

The San Francisco conference opened at 4:30 P.M., April 24, 1945, in the War Memorial Opera House. United States Secretary of State Edward R. Stettinius, Jr., opened the conference as temporary chairman. Stettinius, who had recently succeeded the ailing Cordell Hull as head of the State Department, rapped three times with his gavel to bring the meeting to order and announced that the "United Nations Conference on International Organization is now convened."

Then Stettinius asked the delegates for a moment of silent and solemn meditation. This was followed by a telephone address by President Truman, who spoke from Washington. His words were broadcast to the assembly.

The president's speech concluded, "If we do not want to die together in war, we must learn to live together in peace.

"With firm faith in our hearts, to sustain us along the hard road to victory, we will find our way to secure peace for the ultimate benefit of all humanity.

"We must build a new world—a far better world—one in which the eternal dignity of man is respected.

"As we are about to undertake our heavy duties, we beseech Almighty God to guide us in building a permanent monument to those who gave their lives that this moment might come."

There were 282 delegates at the conference, plus their

extensive staffs. When Truman's broadcast ended, many of the chief delegates made speeches. Most followed the same line, praising the memory of Franklin D. Roosevelt for his work in bringing the conference about, and then speaking feelingly of the need for a peace-keeping organization.

Even V. M. Molotov, the Western-hating people's commissar for foreign affairs and chairman of the Russian delegation, fell into the general line of opening speeches. "Today," he said in part, "as well as on many other occasions, we must remember the great name of President Franklin Roosevelt. His services in the struggle for the achievement of a lasting peace, and in the preparation of this historic Conference, have met with a wide recognition among all the peace-loving nations. . . .

"The Soviet Government is a sincere and a firm champion of the establishment of a strong international organization of security. . . . We will fully cooperate in the solution of this great problem [world peace] with all the other governments devoted to this noble cause."

When the speeches stopped, the fighting began.

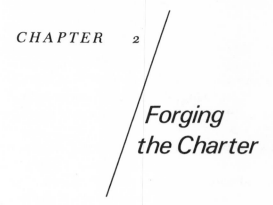

CHAPTER 2

Forging
the Charter

The first fight at the San Francisco conference was over the seating of the two extra Russian delegates from the Ukraine and Byelorussia. South American countries, angered because they had not been consulted on the Dumbarton Oaks agreements, objected strenuously to admitting the two extra Soviet countries as individual members of the United Nations. The United States and Great Britain, bound by their agreements to Stalin, supported Russia, and the Ukraine and Byelorussia were accepted.

Russia next insisted that a delegation from Poland be seated and that Argentina be denied a seat because of her government's sympathy for Hitler. The United States and Great Britain refused to give in to these demands. Poland did not yet have a stable government, but she later solved her political crisis and was admitted in time to be considered a founding nation.

Russia's defeat on the move to deny a seat to Argentina crystallized Molotov's suspicion that the United Nations was dominated by pro-American nations. The Russian foreign minister felt he had a good case for excluding Argentina and took this defeat with ill grace. Argentina had remained neutral during most of World War II, despite the pro-Nazi sentiment of many of her leading politicians. When the Dumbarton Oaks agreement limited UN membership to those nations who declared war on Germany, Argentina hastily declared war to meet the requirements. Molotov had no sympathy for ex-Nazi admirers or for any country that had remained neutral during the war. He very forcefully gave his opinion. The United States, interested in South American solidarity, refused to give in to the Russian.

Both the United States and the other countries of South America strongly supported Argentina. When this battle was won, the Latin American delegates then led a strong fight against the Yalta agreement that permitted any one of the Big Five permanent members of the Security Council to veto the Council's actions. The South Americans argued, with good reason, that the basic principle of the proposed United Nations was equality of nations. They pointed out that the veto permitted any one of the Big Five to stop an action favored by the other fifty members. This, they contended, was hardly equality among nations. They demanded a one-nation, one-vote policy instead.

In the years to come Russia would use the veto power so often that many critics came to believe that the veto had been inserted in the UN Charter at Russian insistence and that the United States and Great Britain gave in to keep Stalin from bolting the conference. This is not true. *All* the Big Five were solidly united against the smaller nations' attack on the veto. Russia wanted the veto in order to be able to stop any action she considered contrary to Communist objectives. The United States feared that the smaller nations might drag her into an undesired war and wanted the veto to stop any such action. France, China, and Great Britain also did not trust the smaller nations and felt that the big powers needed some kind of brake to prevent small nations from ganging up and telling the big powers how to run their business.

Enrique Garcia of Mexico summed up the small nations' opinion of the veto by saying, "What we are creating here is a system of order in the forest which will keep the mice in order, but not the lions." In effect that was exactly what the Big Five had in mind.

The debate went on. Senator Tom Connally of Texas, one of the United States delegates to the conference, used dramatics to underscore the Big Five's position. Connally was then chairman of the Senate Foreign Relations Committee and a man who would have great influence when the Charter came up for ratification by the U.S. Senate. Connally looked like a cartoonist's conception of a senator. He was portly, had long hair and heavy jowls, and habitually wore an old-fashioned standup collar with a string bow tie. But he was an extremely shrewd politician. While arguing that the Big Five had the military strength to do what they wished anyway, Connally suddenly picked up a copy of the proposed United Nations Charter and ripped it in half. Then he told the stunned delegates that there would be no Charter if they would not accept the veto.

Just as the small nations were giving in reluctantly on the veto question, Andrei Gromyko, who headed the Russian delegation when Molotov was absent, balked at what he considered an attempt by Republican Senator Arthur H. Vandenburg to water down the veto. Vandenburg, whom Roosevelt had originally appointed to the U.S. delegation in order to obtain Republican support, introduced a resolution to limit the veto to "substantive" matters, but to prohibit it on procedural matters. Substantive matters were defined as actions concerning peace-keeping complaints before the Security Council. Procedural matters were concerned with how the Council organized itself, what subjects it would consider, and how they would be considered.

Gromyko accused the United States of violating the Yalta agreement. The American delegation passed the problem to President Truman, who backed them fully. He realized that if the power of the veto was extended to procedural matters, then any one of the Big Five could prevent the Security Council from accepting or discussing any dispute the objecting member might find embarrassing to it. Truman realized that the smaller nations would never agree to this.

Russia in turn argued that there was great political significance in the discussion of an international dispute. "Therefore," Gromyko insisted, "the question, whether a dispute should be considered, in no way can be deemed a procedural matter."

This deadlocked the conference. Only the Russian bloc stood for extending the veto. The rest of the nations backed the U.S. stand. Gromyko asked Stalin for instruction.

Senator Vandenburg later wrote, "We had been waiting ten days for the reply from Moscow. The answer— Russia demands her 'veto' even on *free speech* in the Council. This collides with the grim conviction of almost every other Power at Frisco. It is 'Yalta' carried to the final, absurd extreme. . . . We all knew that none of us could accept the Soviet view. Did it mean the immediate breakup of the Conference?"

It appeared that it would break up the conference, and maybe kill the idea of a United Nations completely. The

American delegation again appealed to Truman for instruction and was told to stand fast. Truman then sent
word to Harry Hopkins, his personal representative in
Moscow, to bring the matter to Stalin's personal attention,
explaining the American position. "Ask him," Truman
instructed, "whether he fully realizes . . . what effect the
Soviet proposal would have upon the character of the
world organization we are all trying to work out. Please
tell him in no uncertain words that this country could not
possibly join an organization based on so unreasonable an
interpretation of the provision of the great powers in the
Security Council."

Harry Hopkins had been with Roosevelt at the previous
meetings with Stalin and knew the great dictator as well
as any foreigner could get to know a man like Stalin. He
explained Truman's position. Stalin replied that it was of
little matter and that he would give in to the American
position.

There were other objections, but in the end the conference finally settled on essentially the draft Charter agreed
on by the conferees at Dumbarton Oaks, with the voting
agreement from Yalta.

One major addition was embodied in Article 51 of the
Charter at the insistence of South American nations. This
read, "Nothing in the present Charter shall impair the
inherent right of individual or collective self-defense if an
armed attack occurs against a Member of the United Nations, until the Security Council has taken the measures
to maintain international peace and security."

The key words here were "collective self-defense." The
Latin American nations had feared that the Charter
would, in effect, outlaw regional defense pacts. Another
Charter addition was that each member could have five
delegates to the General Assembly, but only one vote. Still
another was the establishment of an International Court

of Justice, which would be the legal arm of the United Nations. However, this court would be virtually powerless unless disputants agreed to accept its rulings. The only way the court's decisions could be enforced would be by action of the Security Council, where the Big Five held a veto.

All the delegates realized that the Charter, as it was finally amended, was far from perfect. When the Charter came up for ratification by the U.S. Senate, Senator Vandenburg—who had been one of the U.S. delegates to the San Francisco Conference—told his colleagues that it was the best that could be achieved under the circumstances.

Another prominent American, Dean Acheson, secretary of state under President Truman, did not participate in the planning of the Charter but was responsible for presenting the Administration's point of view before the Senate Foreign Relations Committee. Acheson wrote in his autobiography, *Present at the Creation:*

> I did my duty faithfully and successfully [in presenting the case for ratifying the Charter], but always believed that the Charter was impracticable. Moreover, its presentation to the American people as almost holy writ and with the evangelical enthusiasm of a major advertising campaign seemed to me to raise popular hopes which could only lead to a bitter disappointment.

The final draft of the proposed Charter provided for a General Assembly which would include representatives from every member nation. Each delegation would have five delegates, five alternate delegates, and as many advisers as it desired. However, each delegation would have but a single vote, regardless of the number of its members.

Questions coming before the General Assembly would

be settled by a two-thirds majority vote on "important questions," and a simple majority would decide other less important questions. The Assembly would decide what questions to place in the "important" category by a simple majority vote.

The exact powers of the General Assembly were spelled out in Charter Articles 9 through 22. In general the articles provide that "The General Assembly may consider the general principles of cooperation in the maintenance of international peace and security, including the principles governing disarmament and the regulation of armaments, and may make recommendations with regard to such principles to the Members or to the Security Council or both."

Article 12, however, puts a restriction on the General Assembly, saying, "While the Security Council is exercising in respect of any dispute or situation the functions assigned to it in the present Charter, the General Assembly shall not make any recommendations with regard to that dispute or situation unless the Security Council so requests."

Owing to the fact that the Charter was written by a committee composed of members of different nationalities, its wording is often confusing. In the case of Article 12, the General Assembly is not permitted to offer advice to the Security Council once the Council has taken a dispute under advisement. At other times the General Assembly can made recommendations or bring disputes to the attention of the Council. However, in matters involving international security, the Charter vests total responsibility in the Security Council. The Assembly's recommendations to the Security Council are suggestions only. These recommendations are not binding on any nation. Only the Security Council can give orders and then back them up by force.

It would appear from this that the Charter vests all authority in the Security Council and that the General Assembly is useless except as a public forum where the smaller nations can put forth their views. And from the standpoint of international security and peace-keeping, this was the plan of the big powers. In time this situation would be modified somewhat, but when the Charter was written, it was plain that the big powers intended to act as Big Brothers to the world.

However, the General Assembly was given other powers not directly associated with the peace-keeping monopoly of the Security Council. These powers, authorized in Article 13 of the Charter, have grown in importance and have brought enormous benefit to the peoples of underdeveloped and developing countries. Nationalist China has been given credit for insisting at Dumbarton Oaks that these responsibilities be included in the Charter.

Article 13 reads,

> The General Assembly shall initiate studies and make recommendations for the purpose of: a. promoting international cooperation in the political field and encouraging the progressive development of international law and its codification; b. promoting international cooperation in the economic, social, cultural, educational, and health fields, and assisting in the realization of human rights and fundamental freedoms for all without distinction as to race, sex, language, or religion.

In time this article would give birth to such tremendously helpful organizations as WHO (World Health Organization), UNESCO (United Nations Educational, Scientific, and Cultural Organization), UNICEF (United

Nation's Children's Fund), United Nations Development Program, and others.

All this, however, was still in the future when at the ninth plenary [full] session of the San Fransisco conference Lord Halifax of Great Britain, the temporary presiding officer, announced: "Now, Ladies and Gentlemen of the Conference, we come to the final action of this, the penultimate plenary session. . . . I feel, Ladies and Gentlemen, that in view of the world importance of this vote that we are collectively about to give, it would be appropriate to depart from the usual method of signifying our feeling by holding up one hand. If you are in agreement with me, I will ask the leaders of the delegations to rise in their places in order to record their vote on an issue [the approval of the UN Charter] that I think is likely to be as important as any of us in our lifetime are ever likely to vote upon.

"If I have your pleasure, may I invite the leaders of delegations who are in favor of the approval of the Charter and the Statute and the Agreement on Interim Arrangements to rise in their places and be good enough to remain standing while they are counted."

The statute referred to by Lord Halifax was the one authorizing and setting the rules for the International Court of Justice. The Agreement on Interim Arrangements dealt with methods of conducting business and arrangements for the first meeting of the United Nations to be held as soon as the Charter was ratified by sufficient nations to put it into effect.

After the chief delegates arose to signify approval, Halifax said, "Thank you. Are there any against?"

No one rose, and the presiding officer said, "The Charter and the other documents are unanimously approved." Immediately everyone in the conference hall at the San

Fransisco War Memorial Opera House rose and cheered. When the cheering subsided, Lord Halifax said, "I think, Ladies and Gentlemen, we may all feel that we have taken part, as we may hope, in one of the great moments of history."

The session was adjourned at 11:15 P.M., to be reconvened the following day, June 26, 1945, at 3:30 P.M. for the official ceremonies when each delegation signed the Charter in the name of its nation. Signing for the United States were Secretary of State Edward R. Stettinius, Jr., Cordell Hull, Senator Tom Connally, Senator Arthur H. Vandenburg, Representative Sol Bloom, Representative Charles A. Eaton, Governor Harold Stassen, and Dean Virginia Gildersleeve.

At the final plenary session all chief delegates took the occasion to make speeches pledging their country's support to the new organization.

Some of their remarks follow:

Stettinius (U.S.): "This is the way of friendship and peace. This is the only way that nations of free men . . . can live at peace with one another."

Wellington Koo (Nationalist China): "It remains for us to continue to foster mutual trust and friendly collaboration in order to make this, the greatest of international experiments, a great success in fact."

Andrei Gromyko (Soviet Union): "When asked whether there is some means of preventing . . . aggression . . . Marshal Stalin gave the following answer: 'To achieve this, there is only one means besides the complete disarmament of aggressor nations: to establish a special organization for defense of peace and insurance of security, from among the representatives of peace-loving nations. . . .' Such are the principles by which the Soviet Government has been guided while taking an active part . . . [in] the work of this Conference."

Lord Halifax (Great Britain): "Here in San Francisco we have seen but the beginnings of a long and challenging endeavor. And there is a sense in which what we have done here is less important than what we have learned here. We have learned to know one another better; to argue with patience; to differ with respect; and at all times to pay honor to sincerity. . . . Time alone can show whether the house that we have tried to build rests upon shifting sand, or, as I firmly hope, upon solid rock, to stand a shield and shelter against every storm."

Harry S. Truman, president of the United States, in a personal address to close the conference: "The Charter of the United Nations which you have just signed is a solid structure upon which we can build a better world. History will honor you for it. Between the victory in Europe and the final victory in Japan, in this most destructive of all wars, you have won a victory against war itself."

And on it went, with each delegation chief adding his thoughts. Time would show that many of the speakers, even if honest in their expressions, did not reflect the true opinions of their governments. And the United Nations became a battleground of ideologies and national selfishness.

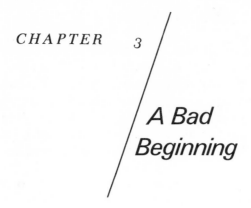

CHAPTER   *3*

A Bad Beginning

Paragraph 3, Article 110 of the UN Charter specified that "The present Charter shall come into force upon the deposit of ratifications by the Republic of China, France, the Union of Soviet Socialist Republics, the United Kingdom of Great Britain and North Ireland, and the United States of America, and by a majority of the other signatory states."

The United States Senate is required by the Constitution to "advise and consent" to U.S. treaties. After considerable debate, the Charter ratification came to a vote on July 28, 1945, with the following resolution:

> *Resolved (two-thirds of the Senators present concurring therein),* That the Senate advise and consent to the ratification of . . . the Charter of the United Nations, with the Statute of the International Court of Justice annexed thereto, formulated at the United Nations Conference on International Organization and signed at San Francisco on June 26, 1945.

The President *pro tempore* of the Senate, after the reading of the resolution, said, "The question is on agreeing to the resolution of ratification. The yeas and nays have been ordered and the clerk will call the roll."

The roll call of votes showed eighty-nine yeas, two nays, and five Senators not voting. This was reported to the chamber, and the president *pro tempore* said, "Two-thirds of the Senators present concurring therein, the resolution of ratification is agreed to, and the treaty is ratified."

Senator Alben Barkley of Kentucky then rose in the chamber to say, "Mr. President [of the Senate], I ask that the President [of the United States] be immediately notified of the action of the Senate in advising and consenting to the ratification of the treaty."

Under the rules the Charter would become effective when a majority of the nations, including all the permanent members of the Security Council, deposited notification of ratification with the United States. The U.S. was the first nation to deposit the ratification. This was done on August 8, 1945. France was second, depositing her ratification on August 31, 1945. The Union of Soviet Socialist Republics was last with a deposit on October 24. This completed the necessary number, and the United Nations was officially proclaimed in a document signed by James F. Byrnes, secretary of state of the United States, who had succeeded Edward R. Stettinius, Jr. After listing the ratifying nations and the dates of their ratification, Byrnes wrote, "Now, therefore, I, James F. Byrnes, Secretary of State of the United States, sign this protocol in the English language, the original of which shall be deposited in the archives of the Government of the United States of America and copies thereof communicated to all the States signatory to the Charter of the United Nations.

"Done at Washington this twenty-fourth day of October, One Thousand Nine Hundred and Forty-five."

The ratification did not put the United States into the United Nations. This was done by the United Nations Participation Act, which the U.S. Senate approved by a vote of 65 to 7 on December 4, 1945, and the House of Representatives approved 344 to 15 on December 18.

This act provided for the president to use American armed forces to cooperate in action with the United Nations against an aggressor. (This was the authority President Truman later used to commit the United States to United Nations action in Korea.) The act also provided for five delegates to the General Assembly and fixed their salaries at $12,000 a year. The United States representative on the Security Council was to receive a salary of $20,000 a year.

Stettinius, who had been secretary of state at the time of the San Francisco conference, was named U.S. representative on the Security Council and one of the five delegates to the General Assembly. The other four General Assembly delegates were Mrs. Eleanor Roosevelt, Tom Connally, Arthur H. Vandenburg and Secretary of State Byrnes.

The appointment of Stettinius shows the inner working of politics in important affairs. Stettinius had been appointed secretary of state by President Roosevelt when Cordell Hull resigned because of ill health. When President Truman succeeded Roosevelt on the latter's death, he wanted his own team and chose Byrnes to replace Stettinius. Because of Stettinius's important position in the Democratic party, it was necessary to find him another major job.

According to an account by Dean Acheson, who later replaced Byrnes, Stettinius's supporters tried to make the UN job even more important than it was. A draft proposal was sent to Truman which gave the chief United Nations delegate a presidential cabinet position. He would be placed on the same level as the secretary of state. Truman sent the memorandum to the State Department for comment.

Dean Acheson wrote: "Mr. Byrnes [the secretary of state], in view of Mr. Stettinius's somewhat ruffled feelings at being summarily replaced, was not inclined to make an issue of it, but I persuaded him that he must do so. The whole integrity of his position was at stake as well as an infinity of trouble over who would be the President's chief adviser and secretary on foreign policy."

Byrnes was able to point this out to Truman, and in the final law the position of the chief U.S. delegate to the UN was accorded ambassadorial rank.

The actual beginning of the United Nations was in London, England, on January 10, 1946, although October 24—the date of international ratification of the Charter—is observed as UN Day. On January 4, Gladwyn Jebb, who was serving as executive secretary of the UN Preparatory Commission to get ready for the opening, sent the following message to all members: "I am desired by Dr. Zuleta Angel, President of the Preparatory Commission, to inform you that the First Part of the First Session of the General Assembly is convoked for 3:45 P.M. on Thursday, 10 January next."

Dr. Eduardo Zuleta Angel of Colombia presided at the opening of the General Assembly, which was in Central Hall, Westminster, London. Dr. Zuleta Angel opened the meeting with a brief address and introduced Prime Minister Attlee of Great Britain. This was followed by the election of Paul Henri Spaak of Belgium to be president of the General Assembly. Trygve Lie of Norway was a strong contender for the presidency but was defeated in the voting by twenty-eight to twenty-three.

The *United Nations World,* an official UN publication, said in a biography of Trygve Lie published in 1947, that the Norwegian was very much disappointed that he did not get elected. "When the United Nations was being organized," the article said, "it was generally considered that the President of the General Assembly would be about the most important man in the world. As it turned out, Lie's disappointment in losing the election turned into an advantage."

This advantage proved to be his consideration for the office of Secretary-General. The Secretary-General is elected by the General Assembly on the recommendation of the Security Council (where the recommendation can be vetoed by any of the permanent members). The Secretary's duties, as outlined in Article 98 of the Charter, are to act in the capacity "of chief administrative officer in all meetings of the General Assembly, of the Security Council, of the Economic and Social Council, and of the Trustee Council, and shall perform such other functions as may be entrusted to him." He can also bring to the attention of the Security Council any matters he feels that are threats to international peace and security.

Since the Secretary-General is permanently on duty and deals with all major organizations of the UN while the president of the General Assembly only presides when the Assembly is in session, the Secretary-General has emerged as the most important and powerful single office in the entire United Nations organization. The importance of the job has been increased by a succession of strong-minded men who held the job and who assumed more responsibility than the framers of the Charter actually intended.

The Secretary-General is elected by the General Assembly from candidates recommended by the Security

Council. No person can be recommended who does not have the unanimous backing of the five permanent members of the Security Council, for the veto would block his recommendation. At the same time the candidate must also have a minimum of four votes from the nonpermanent members of the Council to attain recommendation.

The Security Council meets in secret to consider the nomination of a new Secretary-General. The General Assembly votes on this recommendation in public. However, policy forbids discussion of the nomination in public. The Assembly receives the nomination or nominations from the Security Council and then takes a public vote without argument. This does not mean that backstage politics is not at work. It is, to a tremendous degree. Each faction wants to seat a Secretary-General favorable to it or at least not favorable to opposing sides.

Despite the intention and efforts to keep the backstage maneuvering secret, things have a way of leaking out. The election of the first Secretary-General shows how the big powers block each other. The president of the General Assembly was elected on January 10, but it was another three weeks before the Security Council could compromise on a nomination for Secretary-General. The Soviet Union insisted on Stanoje Simitch, Yugoslavian foreign minister, for the position. (This was before the break between Stalin and Marshal Tito, dictator of Yugoslavia.) Great Britain and the United States flatly refused to agree to a Communist in the Secretary-General's position. Russia in turn rejected Great Britain's suggestion that either General Dwight D. Eisenhower or Britain's diplomat Gladwyn Jebb be considered. France wanted her ambassador to the United States, Henri Bonnet, while the United States backed the nomination of Lester B. Pearson of Canada. Pearson was an extremely able man who commanded world respect.

The Soviet Union refused to accept Pearson. The General Assembly had already voted to make the permanent headquarters of the UN somewhere in North America. For this reason, Russia took the stand that a European rather than a North American should be Secretary-General. The actual reason was that Stalin was extremely suspicious of the British and did not intend to have a member of the British Commonwealth in the office.

The deadlock made it apparent that no member of the Big Five could ever hope to become Secretary-General. The final appointee would have to be from a small country and one who stood midway between communism and democracy. To this end the United States shifted her support to Trygve Lie. After some political maneuvering, the eleven members of the Security Council unanimously agreed on the Norwegian and sent his nomination to the General Assembly. He was elected on February 1, 1946, by a vote of eighty-six to three. The voting was done by secret ballot, and the countries casting the three negative votes were not publicly disclosed.

The new Secretary-General was born in Olso, Norway, in 1896. His father was first a carpenter and then a station master for a railroad until he died when Trygve was a small boy. While still a teenager Lie became office boy in the Norwegian Labor party's headquarters in Oslo and at sixteen headed a branch of the party. He worked his way through law school and became secretary of administration in the Labor party organization. Two years later he accompanied a Norwegian delegation to Russia. On his return he began specializing in labor law, defending pickets who attacked strikebreakers.

Lie then entered local politics. When the Labor party swept into office in 1935 he was made minister of justice and in 1939 minister of shipping and supply. During the war, when Norway was overrun by Germany, Lie was a member of the Norwegian government-in-exile in London. From there he went to San Francisco in April, 1945, to represent the exiled Norwegian government at the conference which adopted the UN Charter. Here he served as chairman of Commission III, which worked out the details for the Charter section on the Security Council and its duties.

The war ended while Lie was in San Francisco, and he returned to Oslo in June, 1945, when the Labor party won a landslide victory in the first postwar election. Lie then became foreign minister and represented Norway in that capacity at the first session of the United Nations in London. After losing the election for president of the General Assembly, he then became Secretary-General when the Security Council accepted him as a compromise nomination. On February 2, 1946, he was presented to the General Assembly and sworn in as Secretary-General by Assembly President Henri Spaak, who enjoined Lie to discharge the functions of the new office "with the interests of the United Nations only in view, and not to seek or accept instructions in regard to the performance of your duties from any Government or other authority external to the Organization."

As a concluding word of advice, Spaak told Lie, "Never lose contact with reality."

There wasn't much chance of that. Lie immediately found himself embroiled in controversy and caught in the middle of a fight between Russia and the democratic members of the Security Council—a fight that would keep the Security Council from ever accomplishing the objectives for which it had been created. The fight among the nations would in time reach the point where Lie himself would come under violent attack and finally be forced to resign. This did not come, however, until after Lie, through his forceful character, turned what could have been a mere administrative and housekeeping position into the most important single job in the United Nations.

The shadow of what was to come became apparent when the Security Council was organized and convened for its first session on January 18, 1946. There were then eleven members. In addition to the five permanent members—China, France, the Union of Soviet Socialist Republics, the United Kingdom, and the United States—the six nonpermanent members were Australia, Brazil, Egypt, Mexico, Netherlands, and Poland. These additional members were elected by the General Assembly.

Work began smoothly. Gromyko of Russia complained because not enough information was available on the revolution in Indonesia where rebel leader Sukarno was trying to oust the Dutch. Then the Security Council participated in the election of judges for the International Court of Justice and began creating a Military Staff Committee. This committee was authorized by the UN Charter to assist the Security Council if it should be necessary to use force to support United Nations demands against an aggressor nation.

Security Council harmony lasted one day. The second day the Council met (January 19) it received a written complaint from the Iranian delegation that Russia refused to remove her troops from Iran's Azerbaijan province. The complaint electrified the small nations, for this was the first real test of the new world organization. It would prove whether a small nation could receive support against one of the world powers. The complaint was received and placed on the Security Council agenda to be heard on January 25.

Russia was outraged at being the first nation to have a complaint lodged against her. Stalin had the Ukraine—

which held a separate membership in the UN—file two complaints against Great Britain. The first claimed that British troops in Greece constituted a threat to international security. The second charge was that British troops sent to Indonesia to receive the Japanese surrender were being used against Indonesian nationalists who were fighting to free Indonesia from the Dutch. The complaint went on to claim that instead of interning Japanese soldiers the British were using the enemy Japanese to fight the Indonesian rebels.

With this action the first showdown in the Security Council moved from the problem of a small nation against a world power to a direct confrontation between two world powers.

In the Iranian dispute Russia announced a willingness to negotiate with Iran, and Andrei Vyshinsky of the Russian delegation insisted that there was no cause for Security Council intervention. The matter was continued with charges and countercharges until Russian troops partly withdrew in May, 1946, and then completely withdrew shortly after. Although UN action was limited to asking the parties to keep negotiating, this was considered a United Nations victory, for it crystallized the full force of world opinion against Russia. The evidence seems to support the belief that Stalin had designs on Iranian oil, and if it had not been for the United Nations, Iran would have fallen into the Soviet orbit.

On the complaint concerning Greece, the Security Council quickly found itself deadlocked. Great Britain insisted, and was supported by the Greek government, that British troops were in Greece with the full consent of the Greek government. Ernest Bevin, British foreign minister, asked for the Security Council to rule that, as British troops would eventually evacuate Greece, their presence at this time did not constitute a threat to peace as the Russians claimed. Andrei Vyshinsky angrily announced that if the Security Council tried to issue such a statement, he would resort to the veto. The deadlock continued for five meetings, and then Stettinius of the United States got Vyshinsky and Bevin to compromise their opposing views. Vyshinsky agreed not to press the Russian claim, and Bevin agreed to withdraw his demand for condemnation of the Russian complaint.

This settled nothing, actually. The so-called compromise was simply that both nations' delegates stopped arguing and the matter went into limbo. The British continued to maintain troops in Greece to protect that country's government from Communist guerrillas. After the guerrilla threat diminished, British troops were withdrawn in 1949—three years after the first Russian demand.

The complaint against British action in Indonesia was something else. Bevin admitted the charge that British commanders were using Japanese war prisoners as soldiers to fight the Indonesian rebels. He claimed that the Dutch were in no position to accept the Japanese surrender in Indonesia at the end of World War II and had asked Great Britain to do so. The British force in Indonesia found itself surrounded and outnumbered by Indonesian rebels trying to break Dutch rule and make Indonesia a republic. The British commander then used Japanese soldier-prisoners to prevent a massacre of the British.

The chief of the Ukraine delegation, who had brought the original charge, demanded that the UN send a commission to Indonesia to investigate the charge and the British defense. Bevin said that any such action would be an insult to His Majesty's government. Then he and Vyshinsky began speaking to each other in the bluntest, most undiplomatic language. Among other things the British foreign minister asked Vyshinsky why Russia and the Ukraine were so concerned when neither Indonesia nor the Dutch had lodged a complaint. The matter stopped here on a deadlock, but the United Nations was not yet rid of the Indonesian problem. It would be back in a short time when guerrilla actions became a full war for independence.

These were the opening skirmishes in what was to be an unending battle among the veto-holding members of the Security Council. In giving five permanent members the veto, it was the stated belief at the San Francisco conference that these nations—having worked together for victory during World War II—would continue to work together for peace. The opening sessions of the Security Council showed that this belief was an idealistic dream. Not one of the five was willing to give up any of its advantages for the sake of international benefits.

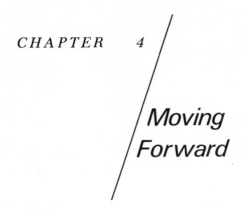

CHAPTER 4

Moving Forward

While the Security Council was bogged down in dissension, the General Assembly moved forward in a most commendable manner. All of the opening months in London were devoted to getting the United Nations organized. Seven committees were established: Political and Security; Economic and Financial; Social, Humanitarian, and Cultural; Trusteeship; Administrative and Budgetary; and Legal. The chairmen of these committees, together with the president of the General Assembly, the Assembly vice presidents, and fourteen members elected at large comprised the seventh committee, which was the Steering Committee.

Next, after joining the Security Council in electing fifteen judges to the International Court of Justice, the Assembly formed an Atomic Energy Commission, came to an agreement on a permanent home for the UN, and went to work on the old League of Nations' problem of the mandated territories.

The mandated territories were former German colonies which had been taken from Germany after World

War I. These areas had been divided among the victorious Allies. Technically they were not given to the ruling nation but were under the authority of the League of Nations, which had given a "mandate" to the occupying nation to govern the mandated territory. The occupying nation was supposed to be responsible to the League for proper administration of the mandates and to make periodic reports. The mandates were in Africa, the Middle East, and the Pacific Ocean area.

With the dissolution of the ineffective League of Nations, the United Nations now proposed to absorb these mandated territories. The occupying nations would continue to govern these areas under a new system of United Nations "trusteeships." However, since the original mandates came from the League of Nations and the United Nations was not a legal successor to the League, the UN had no authority to absorb these mandates unless the occupying governments voluntarily relinquished their League mandates.

Great Britain readily agreed to hand over her three mandates in Africa and to permit mandated Trans-Jordan to form an independent nation, but she balked at giving the UN control in Palestine. Bevin of Britain told the General Assembly that his country wanted more time to study the Palestine question before making a decision. At this time Palestine was Arab-occupied but under British jurisdiction. Great Britain—in accordance with the Balfour Declaration of World War I—was committed to Zionism, or the establishment of a Jewish national homeland in Palestine. The conflict this aroused between Jews and Arabs created problems that still disturb the United Nations and world peace to this day. All the great nations understood the tremendous problems associated with turning an Arab-occupied land into a Jewish state. So there was no objection from any of them when Bevin announced Great Britain's refusal to commit herself on Palestine at this time.

France and the Union of South Africa ignored the UN trusteeship plan. Nor did the United States like it. The U.S. intended to build military bases in the former Japanese mandated islands of the Pacific Ocean. The U.S. military staffs did not want any United Nations trusteeship committee sending observers to check operations in these islands.

A number of important resolutions were passed by the UN. One was for the United Nations to cooperate with UNRRA (United Nations Relief and Rehabilitation Administration). UNRRA was formed before the United Nations organization to aid refugees and displaced persons of World War II. Another resolution had to do with reconstruction of devastated countries. Still another was an invitation to the World Federation of Labor, the American Federation of Labor, and the International Cooperative Alliance to work with the UN Economic and Social Council.

The General Assembly also took note of the war crimes trials which opened in Nuremberg, Germany, in November, 1945, to try high German officials for "crimes against humanity." The United Nations took no part in the actual trials of the Nazi leaders. They were conducted entirely by Great Britain, France, Russia, and the United States. However, the General Assembly adopted a resolution calling on all members "to cause the arrest of those war criminals who have been responsible for or have taken a consenting part in these war crimes, and to cause them to be sent back to the countries in which their abominable deeds were done, in order that they may be judged and punished according to the laws of these countries."

In addition, the resolution called on nations not part of the United Nations to likewise apprehend any war criminals who may have fled to those countries.

In a separate action, supported by the United States and Russia, the General Assembly adopted a resolution refusing membership in the United Nations to Spain, whose Franco government had gained power through aid from Hitler.

Not the least of the General Assembly's tasks was the selection of a permanent site for the United Nations headquarters. San Francisco had been suggested and rejected. Switzerland, because of her traditional neutrality, was favored by some, but the Swiss refused. Switzerland was not a member of the UN and did not intend to become one. She feared that the United Nations requirement for joint action against an aggressor violated the Swiss principle of never siding with either side in an international dispute.

After the decision was made to locate in the United States, the General Assembly agreed to temporary headquarters in New York while a permanent site was being selected. Arrangements were made with Hunter College in the Bronx for space to hold the Security Council meeting of March 25, 1946. Other groups met at various temporary locations. The headquarters selection committee favored building the UN permanent headquarters in either Fairfield County, Connecticut, or Westchester County, New York. Both were rich, exclusive residential sections. The outcry against disturbing them with politicians was loud and telling. The disconcerted committee was about ready to suggest the headquarters be moved out of the United States when Nelson Rockefeller (later governor of New York) persuaded his father, John D. Rockefeller, Jr., to donate $8,500,000 to buy a site on New York's East River.

The first half of the first session of the General Assembly recessed in London in February and reconvened in New York in the Sperry Gyroscope Company plant, Long Island, in October, 1946. One of the most important actions to come from this second part of the first session was unanimous approval of the resolution to establish UNICEF—United Nations International Children's Emergency Fund. (This organization was renamed United Nations Children's Fund in 1953, but the UNICEF designation was retained.) The original purpose of UNICEF was to provide food, medical attention, and clothing to needy children in postwar reconstruction. When this was completed in 1950, the UN voted to broaden UNICEF's activities to include children of underdeveloped countries of the world.

In rapid actions the General Assembly also:

•Adopted an official UN seal (a polar projection of the world map encircled by olive leaves).

•Approved sentences given at the Nuremberg war crimes trials.

•Requested South Africa to give better treatment to Indian minority groups.

•Passed a resolution inviting nations to pass laws prohibiting genocide—mass murder of racial or religious groups.

•Approved agreements to incorporate certain international organizations into the UN's Economic and Social Council as specialized agencies. These included UNESCO (UN Educational, Scientific, and Cultural Organization); Food and Agriculture Organization; International Labor Organization; and the Provisional International Civil Aviation Organization.

•Approved eight trustee agreements for members to govern nongoverning areas (former mandates). They assigned New Guinea to Australia; Ruanda-Urundi (Africa) to Belgium; Cameroons (Africa) to France; Togoland (Africa) to France; Western Samoa (Pacific) to New Zealand; Tanganyika (Africa) to Great Britain; Cameroons (British area, not to be confused with the French Cameroons) to Great Britain; and British Togoland also to Britain.

•Approved reports that would lead to formation of the World Health Organization.

•Admitted—with Security Council approval—Thailand, Afghanistan, Iceland, and Sweden as new UN members and sent a resolution to the Security Council asking reconsideration of the membership applications of Ireland, Portugal, and Trans-Jordan after these three nations were rejected because of a Russian veto.

This flurry of work was all accomplished within two months, ending with the adjournment of the General Assembly on December 15, 1946. Assembly president Paul Henri Spaak congratulated the delegates on the monumental amount of work accomplished and said, "We are all exhausted." No one disagreed. Spaak then announced that the next session would convene in October, 1947. As it happened, the delegates were back in New York much sooner than they had expected. A special session was called in April, 1947, when Great Britain gave up trying to find a solution to the impossible situation in Palestine and threw it into the United Nations' lap.

Before this happened, the Security Council became bogged down again in a three-cornered fight among Russia, France, and Great Britain. Syria and Lebanon complained early in 1946 that France and Great Britain still had occupation troops in their nations. The Security Council considered the problem and approved a resolution requesting France and England to remove their troops. The resolution was vetoed by Russia's Andrei Vyshinsky on the peculiar grounds that the resolution did not brand France and Great Britain as "imperialist aggressors." Despite the Russian veto, Great Britain and France chose to heed the majority Security Council vote and agreed to withdraw their occupation troops.

The next crisis in the Security Council came in December, 1946, when the Greek government charged that Communist guerrilla raids on Greek frontier settlements from Albania, Bulgaria, and Yugoslavia had reached the proportions of an actual invasion. A Commission of Investigation, under direction of UN Secretary-General Trygve Lie, supported the Greek claim. The accused governments—Albania, Bulgaria, and Yugoslavia—angrily denounced the Commission, claiming that all the disturbance in Greece was due to the presence of British troops. When the Security Council drafted a resolution calling on the three Balkan countries to stop supporting the guerrilla attacks on Greece, Andrei Gromyko—the Russian delegate—vetoed the resolution.

This crisis became a milestone in United Nations history, because it brought about the first determined attempt to circumvent the paralyzing vetoes used by the Russian delegation to block the majority of Security Council actions since the first session in London. After several months of trying to come to an agreement with the Russians and getting nowhere, Hershel Johnson—then the U.S. delegate—suddenly moved that the Greek problem be dropped by the Security Council, since no progress was being made.

On the surface this appeared to be acknowledgment of defeat, but it was not so. The UN Charter restricted the General Assembly from "offering advice or comment" while a security problem was under consideration in the Security Council. By discharging the complaint in the

Council, Hershel Johnson knew that it could then be discussed in the General Assembly. The Assembly, of course, could not take any binding action against Albania, Bulgaria, and Yugoslavia. Enforcement action could only be taken as a result of a Security Council motion, which was impossible because of the Russian veto. However, those supporting Greece hoped that open debate in the General Assembly would focus world disapproval on Russia and that this disapproval would cause Stalin to stop supporting the guerrillas attacking Greece.

The presidency of the Security Council rotated among the members, and Gromyko was president when Hershel Johnson made his motion to discharge the Greek problem. Gromyko refused, threatening to veto any such action. Johnson retaliated by claiming that a motion to discharge was a matter of procedure. It will be remembered that when the UN Charter was being hammered out, Russia demanded the right to veto even the discussion of a problem in the Security Council. President Roosevelt balked at this violation of free speech, and Stalin reluctantly gave in, saying it was unimportant. It was agreed that substantive matters relating to complaints and security would be subject to the Five-Power vetoes, but that procedural matters involving how an issue should be considered would not be subject to veto. Now this agreement was working to Russia's disadvantage.

Gromyko violently rejected Johnson's claim that dismissal of the Greek complaint was a matter of procedure. He claimed it was a substantive part of the security complaint. As the president of the Security Council, Gromyko made a ruling upholding his interpretation of the Charter. Johnson immediately challenged the ruling and demanded a vote. The majority of the Security Council sided with the United States view, voting that discharge of the Greek question was a matter of Council procedure. This Russian defeat was followed by another when the Council—as a matter of procedure—passed a resolution asking the General Assembly to consider the problem of Greece and her neighbors.

Shifting the problem to the General Assembly did not solve it. All the Assembly could do was debate the problem and call on the countries involved to settle their differences. However, as Johnson and the supporters of Greece had hoped, moving the problem into the Assembly was a major victory in that it brought all facets of the problem to public attention throughout the world, damning Albania, Bulgaria, and Yugoslavia, along with Russia, who supported them. It also brought a strong attack on the veto system by various delegates who spoke strongly in Assembly speeches against the way the veto was being used to hamper international settlements.

Russia did not give up without a fight. Andrei Vyshinsky led the Russian delegation denunciation in the Assembly. Vyshinsky had been Stalin's prosecutor-general in the infamous Moscow treason trials of the late 1930s and was known for making speeches that turned into tirades. The fight continued through 1947 before the Assembly was able to get through a resolution calling on Greece, Albania, Bulgaria, and Yugoslavia to make every effort to settle their differences. The resolution also called on the three Balkan countries to stop aiding the guerrillas and to set up UNSCOB (United Nations Special Committee on the Balkans).

Whether these actions would have had a practical value in stopping the aggression against Greece is doubtful. Greece was saved by two things. One was continued United States and British military support. The other was a falling out between Marshal Tito and Russia. This removed Yugoslavia from the direct political control of Stalin. Tito, the Yugoslavian dictator, then became involved in a quarrel with Bulgaria, which disrupted each country's support of the guerrillas in Greece. Russia was reluctant to aid guerrilla action in Greece for fear Tito would emerge the victor if the Greek government was overthrown. So the Greek problem gradually wound down and by 1949 had ceased to be a threat to international security.

In the meantime the Security Council was mired in other problems. Of these the most crucial at the time was the Palestine question. The problem itself is ages old, but the present situation began in November, 1917, when Arthur James Balfour, British foreign secretary, issued the Balfour Declaration in which Great Britain promised Dr. Chaim Weizmann of the World Zionist Organization that Great Britain would support the establishment of a national Jewish homeland in Palestine. The Declaration specified that the establishment of such a Jewish nation would not endanger the civil and religious rights of any non-Jewish groups in Palestine, nor would this affect the citizenship of Jews in any other country.

At the time of the Balfour Declaration, Palestine was in the hands of the Ottoman Turks, who were allied with the Germans in fighting the British. The British had enlisted Arab aid in fighting the Turks. The famous Lawrence of Arabia (T. E. Lawrence) was detailed to join the Arabs and organize guerrilla bands to support an invasion by General Edmund Allenby of the British Army. Those who fought so valiantly with Lawrence did so with the understanding that after the Turks were routed Palestine would revert to the Arabs. Some Arab leaders were already envisioning a united Arab republic that would stretch from Syria and Iraq, touching the Turkish border down through Lebanon, Palestine, Jordan, Saudi Arabia, and into Egypt.

What the British had done, in effect, was to pledge Palestine to both the Arabs and the Jews, which caused one sarcastic observer to refer to Palestine as the "Twice-Promised Land." Caught in this dilemma, the British were unable to make good on either promise. At the end of the war Great Britain assumed responsibility for Palestine under a League of Nations mandate signed July 24, 1922. Although Article 2 of the mandate agreement specified that Great Britain would "secure the establishment of the Jewish National Home," nothing concrete was done to implement it until 1937, when the Peel Commission recommended that Palestine be partitioned between Arabs and Jews.

Finally, in an attempt to appease the Arabs and to cut down on fighting between Arabs and Jews, Great Britain cut Jewish immigration into Palestine to 75,000 a year for the next five years. When this order expired in 1944, all Jewish immigration into Palestine would stop unless the Arabs agreed to additional Jewish immigration. Four months after this declaration was issued, World War II broke out, in September, 1939, freezing the Palestine question until the war ended in 1945. At this time there were hundreds of thousands of Jewish refugees crying for immigration rights to Palestine, and agitation for the Jewish homeland promised in the Balfour Declaration reached new heights.

The struggle between Jews and Arabs in Palestine reached the point where Great Britain, unable to reach a compromise between the two, informed the United Nations on April 2, 1947, that the situation was beyond her control and asked for a special session of the General Assembly to consider the Palestine problem and the question of its future government. This was the first special session of the General Assembly, and it convened at Flushing Meadow, New York.

It is very seldom that a great nation voluntarily gives up any territory that it has acquired. In the case of Palestine, the British turned their mandate over to the United Nations willingly and with great relief. Their twenty-five years in Palestine had brought them nothing but grief and had been a total failure. The British had gone into Palestine at the end of World War I with the belief that they came as liberators to wipe away the injustices of long Turkish rule. Instead they found that they had to keep an army on constant alert to prevent the Palestinian Jews and Arabs from destroying each other.

Despite a quarter century of effort, the differences between the two Palestinian groups were irreconcilable. Britain's bitterness over the Palestine situation was clearly brought out in a statement made to the Security Council in April, 1947, when the problem was shifted to the General Assembly: "We hope by our withdrawal and relinquishment of authority, that the naked realities of the situation would be better appreciated by all concerned. British administration of the [Palestine] mandate has brought down upon our heads the execration of the Jews and the bitter resentment of the Arabs; it has made us the butt of malicious criticism throughout the world. We have played our part to the limit of our resources." May 15, 1948, was set as the date of withdrawal. This gave the United Nations thirteen months to find a solution to a problem that had frustrated the British for twenty-five years.

The special session of the General Assembly, called by Secretary-General Trygve Lie, at Great Britain's request, met for eighteen days, adjourning on May 15, 1947. The problem to be considered was who would govern Palestine when the British withdrew. The alternatives were to give the mandate to another major nation; to create two separate nations of Jews and Arabs; and to create a federal state composed of one Jewish and one Arabic state within the union. After hearing representatives from both the Jewish Agency for Palestine and the Arab Higher Committee of Palestine, the Assembly voted to form a United Nations Special Committee on Palestine (UNSCOP). The Assembly deliberately excluded members of the Big Five from the committee, choosing members from Australia, Canada, Czechoslovakia, Guatemala, India, Iran, Netherlands, Peru, Sweden, Uruguay, and Yugoslavia.

Committee members visited Palestine, Lebanon, Syria, Trans-Jordan, and Jewish refugee camps in Austria and Germany before going to Geneva, Switzerland, to write a final report. On August 31, 1947, the committee recommended to the General Assembly that Palestine be divided into a Jewish state and an Arab state with Jerusalem as a special international city beyond the jurisdiction of either. These three territories would then be linked together into a single economic unit.

The plan was submitted to a vote and passed thirty-three to thirteen, with ten nations abstaining from the voting. The British mandate would end May 15, 1948, and the last British troops would be withdrawn from Palestine by August, 1948. The Jewish and Arab states would come into being two months after the withdrawal of British troops, and the United Nations trustee committee would make plans for governing the international city of Jerusalem. The Security Council was asked to keep watch for any breach of security that might result from the partitioning of Palestine. In doing this, the General Assembly made it plain that any attempt by either Jews or Arabs to change the borders set by the partition resolution would be considered an act of aggression and a threat to world peace within the meaning of the United Nations Charter.

Since the General Assembly has no power to enforce any order, the problem of securing obedience to this resolution had to be shifted back to the Security Council. Here the problem rested at the end of 1947. If the General Assembly had any illusions about the success of its partition plan resolution, the British certainly did not. They had spent twenty-five years trying to reconcile the warring groups in Palestine and knew that chaos would follow the pullout of British troops from the Holy Land.

Even so, the British were determined to leave.

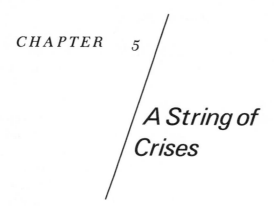

CHAPTER 5

A String of Crises

While the General Assembly was struggling with the Palestine partition problem, the Security Council faced a new series of international problems.

One of these was the "Indonesian Question." At the end of World War II, Indonesian rebels declared their independence from the Netherlands. The Dutch had controlled the Indonesian islands from the seventeenth century when their merchants first began exploiting the famous spice islands. The war between the Dutch and the Indonesian rebels supposedly ended in November, 1946, with the signing of the Linggadjati Pact.

This agreement recognized Indonesia's independence. It provided for the creation of three states: the Republic of Indonesia, Borneo, and the Great East. (The Great East would encompass the Indonesian islands east of Borneo.) These three states would become members of a federation to be called The United States of Indonesia. The federation and the Netherlands would then become equal partners in a Netherlands Union which would handle economic and international politics for the union.

However, the Linggadjati Pact did not end the fighting, which increased in fury as Sukarno attempted to force the Dutch completely out of the Far East. Finally India and Australia complained to the Security Council on July 30, 1947, that the situation in Indonesia threatened international peace. Two days later the Security Council (agreeing for once) issued a call for a cease-fire in the Indonesian fighting. This was followed by the creation of a "good offices" committee to help bring the Dutch and Indonesians together. The Good Offices committee brought about the Renville agreement—so-called because it was signed aboard the U.S.S. *Renville,* a U.S. Navy ship. The agreement recognized Indonesian sovereignty, but provided that the eastern islands of Java, Sumatra, and Madura would have a plebiscite to determine their political future. This agreement was reported to the Security Council on February 10, 1948.

It now appeared that the Security Council was at last functioning as the UN Charter had originally envisioned. The Renville agreement seemed to prove that the Council could be effective—if the problem did not directly involve the interests of the Big Five. If Russia, Great Britain, France, China, and the United States could not work together on their own problems, they could at least work in harmony on the problems of smaller nations.

The peace achieved by the Good Offices committee in Indonesia lasted just one month and nine days. On March 19, Indonesia complained to the Security Council that the Netherlands government had established a State of East Sumatra in violation of the Renville agreement. Efforts of the Good Offices committee to resolve the problem were refused by the Dutch governor, Hubertus van Mook. Later van Mook reluctantly agreed to negotiate. An uneasy truce stretched into December, 1948, when the Good Offices committee reported that the Dutch government

had delivered an ultimatum to the Indonesian government, calling for a surrender to the Dutch position on
every point then in dispute. The Dutch demanded a return to the provisions of the Linggadjati Pact. Indonesia
refused, and Netherlands planes bombed Indonesia and
dropped paratroopers in western Java.

The Security Council issued an emergency call for a
cease-fire and for the release of President Sukarno, who
was being held as a political prisoner. The fighting ceased,
but the diplomatic and political maneuvering continued
until a final settlement was made in November, 1949, at
a conference at The Hague in the Netherlands. The settlement called for the Netherlands to recognize Indonesian
sovereignty over all the Indonesian islands except New
Guinea. New Guinea would remain under Dutch control,
pending further developments. While the final agreement was made by direct negotiations between Indonesia
and the Netherlands, the United Nations received a major
part of the credit for stopping the fighting and bringing
the two disputants together. In a message to both parties
at the time of the final settlement, Secretary-General
Trygve Lie said, "Once more the United Nations way of
conciliation and mediation has proven its value."

Concurrent with the Indonesian question, the Security
Council also had to contend with the India-Pakistan dispute. This situation was somewhat similar to the Palestine
problem. India was in the process of becoming an independent dominion within the British Commonwealth of
Nations. At the time, India's population included about
230,000,000 Hindus and 90,000,000 Moslems. The Moslems, who were congregated in sections in the east and
west, withdrew from India and formed the nation of Pakistan, which was admitted to the United Nations as a new
state.

A dispute then broke out between Pakistan and India

over the province of Kashmir. Kashmir is an area about the size of Utah which is cut by the Indus River. While quite mountainous (containing Mount Godwin Austen, 28,250 feet, and Nanga Parbat, 26,660 feet), the province is also the site of the fabled Vale of Kashmir. This valley, formed by a tributary of the Indus River, is extremely beautiful and has a mild climate. Kashmir, under terms of the India independence agreement, was supposed to decide by plebiscite if she would join India or Pakistan or remain an independent state.

The Kashmiri people were predominantly Moslem, favoring union with Moslem Pakistan, but the ruling Maharajah, Sir Hari Singh, was a Hindu. While Hari Singh preferred Kashmir to remain independent, he agreed to cede the province to India in exchange for military help against Pakistani tribesmen who invaded Kashmir in October, 1947. The invasion brought India and Pakistan to the point of war. The United Nations succeeded in stopping the fighting, but the basic trouble was not settled. The hate engendered would cause India to invade West Pakistan in 1971.

In February, 1948, the Security Council faced a new crisis in Czechoslovakia. The country's president, Eduard Benes, suddenly resigned, and the foreign minister, Jan Masaryk, plunged to his death from his office window. A Communist regime immediately took over the government. Dr. Jan Papanek, Czechoslovakia's UN delegate, sent a letter to Trygve Lie in March. Papanek claimed that

> one member of the United Nations has violated the independence of another.
>
> The Government of the Czechoslovak Republic . . . has been undermined and openly placed in jeopardy on February 22, 1948, through force by a Com-

munist minority. This Communist minority was encouraged and given promise of help, if necessary, by the representative of the Government of the Union of Soviet Socialist Republics who came to Prague for that purpose, led by V.A. Zorin, Deputy Minister of Foreign Affairs.

The political independence of Czechoslovakia, a member of the United Nations, has thus been violated by threat of use of force of another member of the United Nations, the Union of Soviet Socialist Republics, in direct infringement of . . . the United Nations Charter. . . .

Trygve Lie ruled that since Dr. Papanek had not been appointed UN delegate by the new regime in Czechoslovakia, his request was "nongovernmental" and therefore could not be considered under the Charter, which barred private citizens from making complaints unless backed by their governments.

Lie's ruling was immediately challenged by Chile. Herman Santa Cruz, Chilean permanent delegate to the UN, wrote Lie:

> Without going into the procedure followed by you in relation to the presentation of the permanent representative of Czechoslovakia and without recognizing the character of private person . . . that you believe Jan Papanek represents, I have the honor, in the name of Chile . . . and by personal and direct order of the President of the Republic, to request you to present to the Security Council the situation referred by [Dr. Papanek].

Since this request for Security Council consideration came from a bona fide member, Lie had no alternative but to forward the matter to the Security Council. It was a foregone conclusion that Russia would certainly veto any action against herself, but she could not stop discussion of the matter in the Security Council. Those countries supporting Czechoslovakia hoped that the public discussion would mass world opinion against Russia, causing the U.S.S.R. to withdraw. This was a vain hope. Andrei Gromyko, the U.S.S.R. member of the Security Council, vetoed all attempts of the Council to investigate the situation in Czechoslovakia.

Meanwhile, elsewhere, the situation in Palestine was degenerating into open warfare between the Jews and Arabs. At the same time and even more serious was a direct confrontation between the United States and Russia over Berlin. After World War II the victorious Allies had divided Germany into occupation zones. Berlin, which was inside the Russian zone, was jointly occupied by Russia, France, Great Britain, and the United States. Russia for some time had been trying to force the Western nations to give up their occupation zones in Berlin.

On March 20, 1948, Russia announced that in her view the Western powers had acted in such a way as to forfeit their rights to occupy Berlin. When this was rejected by the Western powers, Russia announced a blockade of the German capital. A currency reform in the Western zone of the city was the announced excuse for the blockade. All roads from the Western occupation zones were closed so that there was no land approach open into the city. This action placed both the German population in the Western sector of Berlin and the Allied occupation troops in danger of starving, as no supplies of any kind were moving into the city from the West.

The United States immediately launched a mammoth airlift to move supplies, including tons of coal, into Berlin by plane. The situation was a showdown, with the strong possibility that a mistake by either side would force a major war. The foreign ministers held a series of meetings to resolve the crisis, but got nowhere.

On September 29, the Western powers called on Trygve Lie to place the Berlin blockade before the Security Council, claiming that it was a threat to international peace. Gromyko objected violently, but since the discussion was a procedural matter, he was voted down. The Soviet delegation then refused to take any part in the discussions. On October 22, the Security Council drafted a resolution requesting the Soviet Union to lift the blockade and to negotiate with the Western powers. The resolution was promptly vetoed by the Russian delegate.

When the office of Secretary-General was set up, framers of the United Nations had envisioned the job as purely administrative. However, Trygve Lie was a strong man who had no intention of taking a back seat, and under his forceful direction the Secretary-General position had increased in importance. Once when the Security Council was debating the Greek question in 1946, Lie threatened to send his own personal fact-finding group to Greece if the Security Council kept dragging its collective feet. He justified this by claiming that the UN Charter required the Secretary-General to bring any international threat to peace to the attention of the Security Council. Therefore, he had the right to make investigations of possible peace threats on his own initiative in order to see if he should call matters to the Council's attention. Lie had been a labor lawyer before going into politics in Norway and had quite a reputation for finding loopholes in the law. The way he applied this talent to his job in the United Nations did not endear him to the Russians, who decided that one term as Secretary-General was enough for Lie.

Now, in cooperation with Herbert V. Evatt of Australia,

the president of the General Assembly in 1948, Lie wrote a letter to the head of the delegations concerned with Berlin, asking that his letter be forwarded to their governments. He said:

> The United Nations, in the performance of its most sacred mission, is bound to afford its assistance and cooperation in the settlement of a situation the continuation of which involves grave dangers for international peace. . . .
>
> We believe the first step is to resolve the Berlin question. This case is still pending before the Security Council. We believe the history of the Security Council's consideration of this case demonstrates that it can be solved.
>
> Every day that the deadlock over Berlin continues, the danger to the peace and security of all nations continues undiminished. Fear of another war is crippling the effort of all nations to repair the damage of the last war and return once more to the ways of peace. The work of the United Nations as a whole in every field of its endeavor is being delayed and undermined.
>
> We respectfully urge the desirability of immediate conversations and of taking all other necessary steps toward a solution of the Berlin question. . . .
>
> We await an early reply to this communication in order that the members of the United Nations . . . may be informed of the progress in the implementation of the General Assembly's unanimous "appeal to the great powers to renew their efforts to compose their differences and establish a lasting peace."

Immediately after this appeal Russia agreed to a meeting with the Allied nations, and the Berlin blockade was lifted in May, 1949. At the time Lie said, "I am especially happy that this agreement has been reached through the agency of United Nations delegates."

While the negotiations were indeed carried on by the UN delegates of Russia and the United States, the lifting of the Berlin blockade was due primarily to the success of the Berlin airlift, which kept the German capital supplied during the 327-day blockade.

At the close of 1947, the UN General Assembly had adopted the partition plan for Palestine. But as the time drew near for Great Britain to withdraw troops from the Holy Land, it became increasingly apparent that when the British left, Palestine would erupt in violence and bloodshed. Terrorist gangs were already at work. The King David Hotel in Jerusalem was blown up, killing a number of Britons, Jews, and Arabs. The fighting became so general that the Security Council ordered a cease-fire, which was ignored. The situation was serious enough for the UN General Assembly to meet in another special session. Since the Zionists were not satisfied with the partition arrangement and the Arabs were adamantly against the creation of a Jewish state, the United States proposed that the UN set up another trusteeship over Palestine. Knowing the troubles of the British under a trusteeship, the Assembly rejected this idea. Instead, the Assembly voted to appoint a UN mediator for Palestine. The reasoning was that a single mediator might succeed where a committee—arguing among itself—would fail.

The Zionists continued with their plans to create the state of Israel, while the neighboring Arab countries massed armies on their borders, ready to crush the new nation. Their position was simple enough. This had been their land for centuries, and they did not intend to permit it to be handed over to an ancient enemy. If the Jews had a claim on it because they had had a nation there two thousand years ago, then the Dutch had a claim on New York, and Istanbul (Constantinople) should be given back to Italy. Furthermore, they insisted that the United Nations had no authority whatsoever to create a new nation.

The Jewish position was set forth in the proclamation of independence of the state of Israel on May 14, 1948:

> The Land of Israel was the birthplace of the Jewish people. Here their spiritual, religious and national identity was formed. Here they achieved independence and created a culture of national and universal significance. Here they wrote and gave the Bible to the world.
>
> Exiled from the Land of Israel the Jewish people remained faithful to it in all the countries of their dispersion, never ceasing to pray and hope for their return and the restoration of their national freedom. . . .
>
> The recent holocaust, which engulfed millions of Jews in Europe, proved anew the need to solve the problem of the homelessness and lack of independence of the Jewish people by means of the reestablishment of the Jewish State, which would open the gates to all Jews and endow the Jewish people with equality among the family of nations. . . .
>
> It is the natural right of the Jewish people to lead, as do all other nations, an independent existence in its sovereign State.

Secretary-General Trygve Lie had worked hard on the partition plan and believed in it. He was prepared to stand firm against Jewish resentment when Israel only got one-eighth of the land the Zionists wanted, and against the angry Arabs who intended to resist giving any land to the Jews. But Lie was caught in a squeeze when the great powers refused to provide the force necessary to back up the United Nations partition plan. With both Arab and Jewish terrorist groups attacking settlements and a full-fledged war threatening, Great Britain flatly refused to leave troops in Palestine to maintain order. Russia, for once, kept out of an international disturbance. The United States, which had previously urged the UN to take action in Palestine, suddenly claimed that the General Assembly did not have the authority to enforce the partition resolution.

Lie was particularly bitter at the stand taken by the United States. He felt that all his hard and dedicated work for peace in Palestine was being destroyed simply because the United States government was afraid of antagonizing large blocs of voters if the UN took action. Some of Lie's supporters privately claimed that the United States wanted war in Palestine so that the UN could intervene with less chance of angry American voters turning against their government. Lie, in turn, felt so bitter at the poor support he received that he decided to resign as Secretary-General. He was persuaded to change his mind, but shortly had cause to regret it.

On May 15, 1948—the day following the proclamation establishing the state of Israel—Egypt invaded the new nation. Iraq, Lebanon, Jordan, and Syria also declared war. Lie called the Security Council into session. The United States had immediately recognized the new nation of Israel, but at the same time the United States showed a reluctance to take Israel's part in the Security Council debates. This reluctance was due to international politics. The bulk of the American people (and even President Truman himself) favored Israel, but the government was under pressure from both American oil companies with interests in Arabia and the British government to do nothing that would antagonize the Arabs. The British were fearful of losing their own oil interests in the Middle East. Britain was paying subsidies and supplying arms to the Arabs in order to keep these oil concessions.

This combined pressure kept the United States from pushing for immediate UN action. Thus, for two days after the formal fighting began, the Security Council was helpless because of the do-nothing attitude of the United States and Great Britain. In the meantime, Israel was saved by the incompetence of her enemies. Each of the attacking Arab countries was jealous of the other. They failed to coordinate their attacks, and their armies, except for the Jordanian forces, were poorly trained. This permitted Israel to stop the Egyptian attack, but Jordan captured half of Jerusalem before the Jordanian push was halted.

The Security Council finally issued a cease-fire order. It was ignored by both Arabs and Israelis. Two additional appeals to halt the fighting were also ignored by the combatants. On May 27 the Council delivered an ultimatum, threatening to cut arms deliveries to both sides. This threat brought an uneasy truce. The General Assembly then voted to appoint a United Nations mediator to assist the UN Truce Commission which had been established by the Security Council.

Count Folke Bernadotte of Sweden was selected as UN mediator. Bernadotte, a tall, slender man of great natural charm, was president of the Swedish Red Cross and known for his selfless public service. He was a nephew of King Gustav V of Sweden and was a direct descendant of Marshal Jean Bernadotte, a soldier under Napoleon, who became king of Sweden and Norway in 1818. Count Bernadotte left for Palestine immediately after his appointment as UN mediator. He took a fifty-five man staff headed by Dr. Ralph Bunche, an American Negro who had been president of Howard University in Washington, D. C.

In the course of overseeing the Palestine truce, Count Bernadotte and his French assistant, Colonel Andre Serot, were shot by assassins while riding in a jeep through Jerusalem. The killings were attributed to the Stern Gang, an Israeli terrorist group. Moshe Sertok, Israeli foreign minister, apologized to the UN in the name of Israel. The shooting was unfortunate, for it created international resentment toward Israel at a time when the new nation badly needed world support. Count Bernadotte had been highly regarded in Scandinavia, and many influential Scandinavian UN officials never forgave Israel for his death. It is improper to blame an entire nation for the act of a single group, but Major General Carl Von Horn, who later commanded the UN peace force in Palestine, complained that the Israeli government did nothing to punish Bernadotte's murderers. In his autobiography, *Soldiering for Peace,* General Von Horn leaves the impression that this indicated that the Israeli government supported Count Bernadotte's assassins.

About all that can be said in defense of the terrorist gangs is that they offset similar groups from the Arab side. In such actions, as in any kind of war, excesses are committed on all sides.

Bernadotte's plan for permanent settlement of the Palestine problem included giving the Negeb sector of Palestine (a triangular section of land that comprised about one-third of Jewish Palestine) to the Arabs. The loss of Negeb to the Israelis would be offset by giving them the western section of Galilee. This division was based on the number of each nationality who resided in the areas. The proposed loss of Negeb was angrily opposed by the Israelis and was one of the reasons for the attack on Bernadotte, since it would reduce the total Israeli territory by at least two thousand square miles.

Bernadotte was succeeded as UN mediator by Ralph Bunche. Shortly thereafter, fighting broke out in Negeb between Jews and Arabs. Bunche was able to arrange another truce, but only after Israeli troops scored notable victories and the Arab forces nearly collapsed. The fighting petered out in 1949 as one after another of the Arab countries agreed to an armistice. Dr. Bunche received the 1949 Nobel Peace Prize for his work in Palestine, and the general opinion was that he had well earned it. However Dr. Bunche did not achieve a lasting peace, although his truce lasted seven years. The Arabs were dedicated to "driving Israel into the sea" and only awaited the right opportunity.

CHAPTER 6

Human Rights

Settlement of the Palestine question was a cooperative effort of the Security Council and the General Assembly through the UN mediator. While this problem was being solved the General Assembly was busy on various humanitarian programs. Among other things, the Assembly recommended studies to help underdeveloped countries, made plans for increasing world food production, urged technical assistance for economic development of small nations, established a UN Postal Administration, and worked toward increasing educational advancement opportunities in the UN Trust Territories.

However, all these worthwhile accomplishments were overshadowed by approval of the Convention on Prevention and Punishment of the Crime of Genocide on December 9, 1948. The vote was unanimous. The following day the Assembly adopted the equally important Universal Declaration of Human Rights. The voting was not unanimous on the last question. The Russian bloc and the Arab countries abstained. The Arab countries objected to the prohibition of slavery in Article 4, and Russia thought some of the articles (such as Article 9, which outlawed arbitrary arrest, detention, or exile) infringed on her rights in controlling some of her satellite countries.

The genocide question had come up before and had been closely examined. Genocide actually means extermination of a people, as Hitler attempted with the Jews in Germany. For the purpose of the United Nations Convention on Genocide, the term was much more inclusive. According to Article I:

> In the present Convention, genocide means any of the following acts committed with the intent to destroy, in whole or in part, a national ethical, racial or religious group, as such: (a) killing members of the group; (b) causing serious bodily or mental harm to members of the group; (c) deliberately inflicting on the group conditions of life calculated to bring about its physical destruction in whole or in part; (d) imposing measures intended to prevent births within the group; (e) forcibly transferring children of the group to another group.

The Convention's text opens with a reminder that the General Assembly had passed a resolution, dated December 11, 1946, stating that genocide is a crime under international law and contrary to the spirit of the United Nations. While the previous statement was simply a resolution, without binding force, the Convention required that the "contracting parties"—that is, those electing to sign the Convention— "confirm that genocide, whether committed in time of peace or in time of war, is a crime under international law which they undertake to prevent and punish." Then in Article 3, "The following acts shall be punishable: (a) genocide; (b) conspiracy to commit genocide; (c) direct and public incitement to commit genocide;

(d) attempt to commit genocide; (e) complicity in genocide."

Article 4 continues, "Persons committing genocide or any of the other acts enumerated in Article Three shall be punished, whether they are constitutionally responsible rulers, public officials or private individuals."

Other articles enjoined the signing countries to pass necessary legislation to punish genocide in their territories. It added that trial should be by competent tribunal of the state where the crime occurred or "by such international penal tribunal as may have jurisdiction with respect to those Contracting Parties which shall have accepted its jurisdiction."

This last article showed the weakness of the United Nations system. There was no such international tribunal and any punishment of genocide had to be left to an individual country's courts. The International Court of Justice, formed with the United Nations in San Francisco, was—and still is—completely powerless. It can only hear cases between countries, and its decisions are not binding unless the parties involved agree to accept the decisions.

Realizing the inadequacies of both national courts and the International Court of Justice to try and punish genocide cases, the General Assembly, also on December 9, 1948, passed the following resolution:

The General Assembly
Considering that the discussion of the Convention on the Prevention of the Crime of Genocide has raised the question of the desirability and possibility of having persons charged with genocide tried by a competent international tribunal;
Considering that, in the course of development of the international community, there will be an in-

creasing need for an international judicial organ for the trial of certain crimes under international law;

Invites the International Law Commission to study the desirability and possibility of establishing an international judicial organ for the trial of persons charged with genocide or other crimes under international law;

Requests the International Law Commission in carrying out this task to pay attention to the possibility of establishing a Criminal Chamber of the International Court of Justice.

Nothing yet has come of this suggestion, and considering the nationalism rampant in the world today, nothing is likely to come of it.

The Universal Declaration of Human Rights was adopted on December 10, 1945, the day following the voting on the Genocide Convention. It passed by a vote of forty-eight to zero, with the U.S.S.R., the Ukraine, Byelorussia, Poland, Czechoslovakia, Saudi Arabia, and the Union of South Africa abstaining from the voting. Refusing to vote is a way of expressing dissatisfaction without casting a negative vote.

The Declaration was the work of the UN's Commission on Human Rights, established in 1946 under the chairmanship of Eleanor Roosevelt, widow of the late American president Franklin D. Roosevelt. As finally adopted, the Universal Declaration of Human Rights is not a binding treaty, but it is important as the first collective attempt of a group of nations to define human rights. Thirteen years after the Declaration was adopted, Dag Hammarskjöld, then Secretary-General of the United Nations, said, "[The Declaration] has in itself no force of law;

but as a 'common standard of achievement for all peoples and all nations,' it crystallizes the political thought of our times on these matters in a way influencing the thinking of legislators all over the world." It becomes then a blueprint and a challenge for nations to live up to its high ideals.

In urging passage of the Declaration, General George C. Marshall, then U.S. secretary of state, warned the General Assembly in a speech that

> systematic and deliberate denials of basic human rights lie at the root of most of our troubles and threaten the work of the United Nations. It is not only fundamentally wrong that millions of men and women live in daily terror of secret police, subject to seizure, imprisonment, or forced labor without just cause and without fair trial, but these wrongs have repercussions in the community of nations. Governments which systematically disregard the rights of their own people are not likely to respect the rights of other nations and other people and are likely to seek their objectives by coercion and force in the international field.

As an expression of the importance and dignity of man, the Declaration is worth reading in its entirety and will be found at the end of this book.

The Universal Declaration of Human Rights has not, of course, been adopted as international law but serves as a guide to members of the United Nations in promoting national laws insuring these rights to its own people.

Trygve Lie, UN Secretary-General at the time the Declaration was passed by the General Assembly, said of it; "The Universal Declaration of Human Rights . . . is destined to become one of the great documents of history."

Unfortunately, while the United Nations was wrestling with the monumental problem of human rights and making some progress, events were shaping up that would plunge the UN into a shooting war.

CHAPTER 7

*The UN
at War*

"[The Security Council] may take such action by air, sea, or land forces as may be necessary to maintain or restore international peace and security."—Article 42 of the United Nations Charter.

In June, 1950, the United Nations found it necessary to go to war under the provisions of Article 42. This conflict —the Korean War—was fought solely because the Russian delegation was not present to veto Security Council action when the problem came to a vote. The peculiar chain of events that made the Korean War possible began on December 29, 1949, when Yakov Malik of Russia challenged the right of the Nationalist Chinese representative to sit on the Security Council. Instead, the Russian delegate demanded that the representative of the newly proclaimed People's Republic of China be seated.

Legally Yakov Malik (not to be confused with Charles Malik of Lebanon or Adam Malik of Indonesia) had international law on his side. When the United Nations was formed with China as one of the founding nations, the

Kuomintang government of Chiang Kai-shek was China's ruling political force. After a series of military losses, the Kuomintang government completely lost control of the Chinese mainland. Chiang Kai-shek moved his headquarters to Taiwan (Formosa) and kept up the fiction that his government represented all of China, not just the island of Taiwan, the Pescadores, and a few off-shore islands. The victorious Communists then established the People's Republic of China.

Regardless of one's sympathy for Chiang Kai-shek's government, the fact remains that the Communist government of Mao Tse-tung was the legal government of China *even though it took over the country by force.* International law regarding revolutions is a very old and practical one. It can be summed up as saying that all revolutions are illegal in the beginning, and those who engage in revolution are traitors to their legal government. But when the rebels win, they cease to be traitors, for they sweep away the old laws. The former rebels and traitors now become heroes.

In staging a revolution, a rebel group breaks no laws but those of the country in which it is fighting. This is acknowledged by the United Nations Charter, which restricts the UN from interfering in the internal affairs of a nation. The UN is empowered to act only if the disturbance within a country causes or is likely to cause international fighting. Once the rebel government is in charge and changes its laws, its acts are no longer illegal, just as George Washington ceased to be a rebel and became a patriot after the American colonies won their revolution. Once a rebel government is in power, it asks diplomatic recognition from other world governments. This recognition is international acknowledgment of the legality of the rebel government. Communist China had fulfilled these

requirements. The Communist government was in complete charge of the Chinese mainland, governing an estimated 600–800 million people. The Communist government had already received diplomatic recognition from
the Communist bloc of nations as well as from Great Britain, Sweden, Denmark, Norway, New Zealand, Yugoslavia, Israel, and the Netherlands.

When the United Nations was formed, it was not governments but *countries* who became members. The Kuomintang government of Taiwan did not, despite Chiang
Kai-shek's claims, represent the people of the mainland of
China. Although the United States had directly supported
Chiang's long fight against the Communists and had insisted that China be made one of the Big Five in the Security
Council with permanent membership, the Truman administration seems to have recognized the legality of Malik's claim for replacing the Nationalist Chinese delegation with a Communist Chinese delegation. According to
Trygve Lie, the U.S. deputy representative to the UN,
Ernest Gross, told him that the "U.S. regarded [the Nationalist Chinese] credentials as valid, but that it *'would
accept the decision of the Security Council on this matter
when made by an affirmative vote of seven members.'* " In
other words, the U.S. wanted Chiang Kai-shek's representative to remain in the Security Council in preference
to admitting Communist China but would go along with
a majority vote to the contrary.

Malik's December objection was ruled out of order but
was renewed in January, 1950. On January 13 the matter
came to a vote in the Security Council with only Russia,
India, and Yugoslavia voting to oust the Nationalist Chinese and seat the Communist Chinese. At this point Malik
and his staff walked out of the Security Council after de-
claring that the U.S.S.R. would not recognize as legal any

actions of the Security Council as long as the Nationalist Chinese held a seat on it.

The Secretary-General was appalled. While he made no public statement on the controversy, in private Lie supported the Russian position. In his autobiography Lie says, "It was *China,* not Chiang Kai-shek, that belonged in the United Nations." Later he added:

> Another consideration that influenced my judgment was historical. Once before, the world had seen a Communist state—the U.S.S.R.—isolated by the West after a successful revolution. I had always believed that this was a great mistake. . . . Was the free world now going to cut itself off in a similar manner from China and its 475,000,000 people—one-fifth of the world's total population?

Lie now began to step to the front as a crusader for peace. In a speech to the B'nai B'rith in Washington, D. C. on March 21, 1950, the Secretary-General launched what he called "A Twenty-Year Program for Achieving Peace through the United Nations." The speech was a trial balloon for his ideas, which he expanded in a "Memorandum of Points for Achieving Peace through the United Nations." The memorandum contained ten points, the most important of which were

1. Inauguration of periodic meetings of the Security Council, attended by foreign ministers or heads of states (summit meetings).

2. A new attempt at an international control system for atomic energy.

3. A new approach to disarmament.

4. Advancement of dependent, colonial countries to independence.

5. More vigorous use of UN specialized organizations.

This memorandum Lie personally delivered to President Truman in the United States, Premier Bidault of France, Clement Attlee of Great Britain, and Premier Stalin of Russia during an extended trip to Europe.

Vice Premier Molotov replied to the memorandum for Stalin, who sat listening at the meeting with Lie. Molotov angrily denounced the memorandum as "pro-American." Lie asked angrily how Molotov could say that in light of the fact that American newspapers had recently "labeled me as a Stalin agent, pro-Communist, etc., and have demanded that I be 'summarily dismissed.'" Molotov did not reply to this and continued to object to Lie's suggestions for disarmament, for modifying the veto in the Security Council, and on most other points.

In Great Britain Lie also found great opposition to his twenty-year peace plan. Only France and the United States seemed favorable. The General Assembly expressed its opinion in a resolution commending Lie for his initiative and efforts. Lie, in turn, went to work to see if he could iron out the points to which Stalin and Molotov and Ernest Bevin objected. Before this could be done, the United Nations and the world were stunned by the outbreak of war in Korea.

Korea had been a United Nations problem since August, 1945, when Japanese forces surrendered. For purposes of receiving the surrender, Korea was divided at the 38th parallel into a Russian zone to the north and a U.S. zone to the south. This division was not intended to be permanent but was done solely as a matter of convenience. However, it proved to be permanent. Korea had been under Japanese domination since 1910, and the big powers did not consider her in a position to form a stable government. As a result, it was decided at the foreign ministers' meeting in Moscow in December, 1945, to set up a trusteeship over Korea for five years, after which the nation would achieve full political independence.

The trustee idea had to be abandoned because of violent Korean objections. The UN then formed a Temporary Commission on Korea and sent it to Korea to oversee general elections. The Russians refused to permit the commission into North Korea, but an election was held in South Korea on May 10, 1948, for delegates to a constitutional assembly. The assembly convened in July and adopted a South Korean constitution. South Korea then became the Republic of Korea on August 5, 1948. Syngman Rhee, a long-time fighter for Korean independence, became the republic's first president. Just about a month later Russia permitted North Korea to organize a government under the name of the Democratic People's Republic of Korea. Kim Il Sung became president.

The United Nations now had to face the reality of a divided Korea. However, things looked favorable when Russia announced that she was removing her troops from North Korea. The United States then began removing U.S. troops from South Korea. There was hope that this might lead to unification of the two Koreas. Instead, guerrilla warfare broke out along the 38th parallel dividing the Koreas. In August, 1949, the UN commission reported:

> There is much military posturing on both sides of the parallel. This holds a serious danger of provoking open military conflict. . . . Note should be taken of the fact that the North Korean regime recently concluded a treaty with the U.S.S.R. It is reported that an agreement for military aid has been concluded between North Korea and the Chinese Communist forces in Manchuria.

This unstable situation continued until midnight of June 24, 1950, Washington time, when the U.S. State Department received word from U.S. Ambassador Muccio in Seoul, Korea, that North Korean troops had crossed the 38th parallel in force. U.S. Secretary of State Dean Acheson notified President Truman, who was in Independence, Missouri, for a vacation. The president hurried back to Washington. In the meantime the State Department had notified Trygve Lie and requested that an emergency meeting of the Security Council be called for the next day.

Lie, not wanting to take action solely upon the appraisal of the situation by the United States, asked the UN commission in Seoul for a report. The commission's reply verified the attack, which began at dawn on June 25 (Korean time). In a meeting of the Security Council at 2:00 P.M. on June 25, Washington time, Lie read the telegram he had received from the UN commission, adding, "The present situation is a serious one and is a threat to international peace. The Security Council is, in my opinion, the competent organ to deal with it. I consider it the clear duty of the Security Council to take the step necessary to reestablish peace in that area."

The Russian delegation was not present and could not veto the resolution, which called for "immediate cessation of hostilities and a return to the 38th parallel of North Korean troops." Dispatches received from the UN commission in Seoul the next day indicated that the UN Security Council cease-fire demand had been ignored. The report also said the North Korean attack was well planned and must be considered a full-scale invasion.

As the invading army moved toward Seoul, South Korea's capital, the United States Air Force flew in transport planes to evacuate Americans from the capital. When North Korean planes menaced the transports, an accompanying flight of protective fighter planes drove off the attacker. One North Korean plane was shot down and an

Air Force major, James W. Little, was credited with firing
the first American bullet of the war.

By June 27, it was clear that South Korea would be
overrun in a few days unless help was given. Accordingly,
President Truman used a sentence in the original Security
Council cease-fire demand as authority to send U.S. Air
Force and Navy units to help the South Koreans. The
sentence asked "all members [of the UN] to render every
assistance to the United Nations in execution of this resolution."

Just before the Security Council was to meet on June
27 to consider what to do about the Korean crisis,
Trygve Lie attended a luncheon where Yakov Malik, the
Russian delegate, was also a guest. Malik was still boycot-
ting the Security Council because of the presence of the
Nationalist Chinese on the Council. Lie invited Malik to
come back and participate in the crucial meeting. Malik,
Lie reports, refused. His absence permitted the Security
Council to pass a new resolution urging all members of
the United Nations to furnish help to South Korea. The
request called for armed assistance "as may be necessary
to repel the armed attack and to restore international
peace and security in the area."

Lie worked hard, addressing personal appeals to indi-
vidual nations to supply troops for the "police action" in
Korea. The United States, on June 27, 1950, committed air
and ground troops to help South Korea, but only Great
Britain, Australia, Canada, New Zealand, Turkey, the
Philippines, the Union of South Africa, France, Belgium,
Holland, Colombia, Ethiopia, Thailand, Luxembourg, and
Greece sent fighting troops. Denmark furnished a hospital ship, and India sent a field ambulance unit. Norway
and Sweden furnished a hospital group each. However,
the United States furnished fifty percent of the fighting

men. South Korea made up a third. The rest came from the other nations.

On July 3, Arne Sunde of Norway introduced a resolution in the Security Council requesting the United States to take over direction of all United Nations forces in Korea and suggesting that such forces display the United Nations flag. The resolution was adopted on July 7, along with an amendment requesting the United States to appoint a Supreme Commander of United Nations Forces in Korea. The next day President Truman announced that General Douglas MacArthur had been appointed Supreme Commander.

MacArthur, son of General Arthur MacArthur, a Civil War hero and former chief of staff of the U.S. Army, was one of the great generals of American history. At the same time he was possessed of a colossal ego that would brook no interference with his will—not even from the president of the United States. Douglas MacArthur had scored the highest marks ever made at West Point and then went on to become the nation's youngest general in World War I. After the war he rose to be Army chief of staff as his father had been before him. He retired from the Army and accepted the position of field marshal in the Philippine Army in order to build up their armed forces before the Philippines gained independence from the U.S. He was still in the Philippines when World War II broke and was called back to the U.S. Army to become commander-in-chief of U.S. forces in the Southwest Pacific.

Article 47 of the UN Charter provides for the establishment of a Military Staff Committee to "advise and assist" the Security Council on military requirements necessary to preserve peace, saying, "The Military Staff Committee shall be responsible under the Security Council for the strategic direction of any armed forces placed at the disposal of the Security Council."

There is no indication on anybody's part that General MacArthur ever paid the slightest attention to the Military Staff Committee. He was under the direct command of the Joint Chiefs of Staff of the United States military establishment and of President Harry S. Truman. All agree that they found MacArthur a difficult and insubordinate person. At one time the Pentagon had a special department to reword orders to MacArthur in the most diplomatic language.

The Korean War opened with United Nations troops being pushed back until they held only a small area known as the "Pusan beachhead," after the South Korean port city. The South Korean troops had not been given adequate weapons, and the American forces were also inadequately equipped. It appeared as if the United Nations might lose its first war. However, as the North Korean army became overextended in moving so far down the Korean peninsula, MacArthur pulled a brilliant maneuver. Making an amphibious end run around the North Korean army, he staged a landing at Inchon, just below the 38th parallel. Inchon, because of high tides and poor landing beaches, was considered an impossible site for a counterattack, and the maneuver was opposed by the army staff in Washington. MacArthur got his way and the attack went off brilliantly, resulting in one of America's great victories.

Dean Acheson, then U.S. secretary of state, insists that the victory was an accident, but general military opinion is against Mr. Acheson, who is not a MacArthur admirer. Trygve Lie, in his autobiography, calls MacArthur a "great man." In any event, the landing at Inchon by units of the U.S. Marines and the U.S. Army drastically changed the situation in Korea. The North Korean invading army collapsed. Large groups surrendered and others began a disorganized retreat north.

Up to this point politicians had left MacArthur alone. The United Nations was losing, and it was well to let MacArthur take the blame. The reversal of the war that followed the Inchon landing brought politics back into the picture. The big question was, "Should MacArthur be ordered to stop pursuit of the invaders when the North Koreans retreated across the 38th parallel?" The Inchon landing began September 15, 1950, and by the beginning of October MacArthur was ready to push into North Korea.

There was strong sentiment for the UN to stop once the North Koreans were out of South Korea. Dean Acheson said, "The Policy Planning Staff . . . argued that General MacArthur should be directed to announce, as UN commander, that his troops would not cross the 38th parallel." Then Acheson, in a talk to the Newspaper Guild, added that the UN objective was to push the North Koreans back to the 38th parallel and restore Korea to the status it had before the beginning of the aggression.

Later a UN official, talking off-the-cuff to reporters covering the subsequent peace talks, said that at this time Chou En-lai of Red China offered to negotiate a "reasonable peace settlement" based on retaining the 38th parallel frontier. This source claimed that Great Britain—through Ernest Bevin—objected strongly, feeling that this was the time to reunite Korea under the South Korean government of Syngman Rhee. Whether this was true or not, the decision was made to continue the war. There was no major objection from any of the United Nations except those of the Russian bloc.

So despite the previous public announcements of Dean

Acheson that the objective was to stop at the 38th parallel, General MacArthur received a personal note from General George C. Marshall to go all the way to the Yalu River, the border between North Korea and Manchuria. It proved to be a tragic decision.

Yakov Malik, the Russian delegate to the Security Council, ended the Soviet boycott of the Council on August 1, and from then on used every parliamentary tactic to tie up Security Council action on the Korean War. The boycott leaves some curious questions unanswered. Russia under Stalin was an absolute one-man dictatorship. The UN boycott could not have been taken by Malik without orders of Stalin. It was continued even after Trygve Lie informed Malik that the Security Council was meeting to consider the Korean problem. The failure of the Russians to attend and cast a veto vote permitted the United Nations to enter the Korean War. This has been called a monumental Soviet blunder. Yet, Stalin was well aware of what was happening and still did nothing. It appears that the Russian dictator wanted the United Nations to commit itself to the war. Why? Perhaps he thought the North Koreans, with the advantage of surprise, could push the United Nations forces into the sea.

President Truman's actions made it plain that the United States would support South Korea regardless of United Nations action. Stalin may have thought that this would cause the rest of the UN to blame the United States for the trouble. This, of course, is conjecture. No one—as Khrushchev made plain after Stalin's death—was trusted by the Russian dictator, and no one knew exactly what Stalin thought. In any event, Stalin could have prevented the UN vote to support South Korea if he had been so minded.

Malik, after returning to his seat on the Security Council, claimed that the Security Council vote to support South Korea was illegal because Russia had not voted. He claimed this failure to vote was an automatic veto. Trygve Lie insisted that the absence of the Russian vote was the same as an abstention. The argument deadlocked the Security Council but did not affect the course of the fighting in Korea. Since the Security Council had committed UN troops, nothing but a Security Council vote could remove them. Such a removal would be subject to veto, and the United States, China, France, and Great Britain —all holders of veto powers—favored UN intervention.

While the Security Council fought a private war among its members, the Korean fighting took an ominous turn. MacArthur's troops drove all the way to the Chinese border at one point. On October 26, 1950, a Sixth South Korean Division regiment was wiped out by a force reported to be Chinese troops from across the Yalu River in Manchuria. The Sixth U.S. Cavalry was reported attacked the next day by similar Chinese troops. MacArthur reported, "Men and materiel in large numbers are pouring across . . . from Manchuria . . . threatening the ultimate destruction of my forces. . . ."

The attacking forces were "Chinese volunteers," as Peking called them. A MacArthur counterattack failed and by December 26, UN forces had been pushed back below the 38th parallel. Seoul was again in enemy hands, and the fighting line was at Wonju in South Korea. Russian-built MIG–15 fighter aircraft had entered the war.

President Truman, in a press conference, said that the United States had no intention "of abandoning the United Nations mission in Korea." In answer to a question, he replied, "Yes, there had been active consideration of the [atomic bomb's] use in Korea."

This frightened Clement Attlee, British prime minister,

so much that he rushed to Washington for a showdown with Truman. The U.S., to quiet Attlee's fears, agreed not to broaden the war without consulting Great Britain. According to Dean Acheson, Attlee was so eager for peace in Korea that he was willing to give Red China Formosa, all of Korea, and a seat in the United Nations in exchange for an end to the war. Attlee believed this to be the only alternative to full-scale atomic war.

While this was going on, the Security Council and the General Assembly were involved in a separate struggle over the Secretary-General's office. Trygve Lie's appointment was about to end, and the stage was set for another East-West confrontation as the fight started to name Lie's successor.

CHAPTER 8

The Trials
of a
Secretary-General

The UN Charter sets the term of office for the Secretary-General at five years. Trygve Lie's term was due to expire February 1, 1951. In 1949 Lie was told by a Soviet delegate that Lie was Russia's choice for a second term. However, the Secretary-General's role in the Korean War operations had infuriated Stalin. Russia's Vyshinsky made it plain that Russia would use the veto to prevent Lie's being elected to a second term. Although Lie was backed by the United States, France, and Great Britain, the Soviet veto would be sufficient to defeat him. Lie's attitude toward Taiwan had alienated Chiang Kai-shek, but United States pressure caused Nationalist China to agree not to oppose Lie's reelection.

Knowing the Soviet attitude toward him, Trygve Lie had no expectation of continuing in office and had earlier made a public statement that he was not a candidate to succeed himself. Despite this attitude in public, Lie was obviously reluctant to quit under fire. Having come up through the hard-hitting labor union movement in his native Norway, Lie was not a man who gave up easily in a fight. However, the situation developed to the point where he wrote a letter which he intended to mail to all members of the Security Council who would have to pass on his nomination before it could be considered by the General Assembly. In the letter Lie mentioned his previous statement that he was not a candidate and added, "I wish to inform you that my position in this regard has not changed." He preferred to bow out rather than give his enemies an opportunity to say they had defeated him.

He showed a draft of the letter to Ernest Gross of the U.S. delegation, who expressed great concern, advising against Lie sending the letters. "It will make our work much more difficult," Gross said cryptically. This seemed to imply that some backstage maneuvering was going on. As a result, Lie decided to sit tight and see what would happen.

Since there was no chance of avoiding a Soviet veto, Lie's supporters came up with a parliamentary trick. They suggested that the Secretary-General's term of office be extended for two years. An extension would not be a reelection. Malik of Russia lodged an immediate objection. He pointed out that Article 97 of the UN Charter required Security Council concurrence for appointment of a Secretary-General. Furthermore, he argued, the term of office had been set in the Charter at five years. An extension of the term would be illegal without amending the Charter.

Malik then proposed the name of Zygmunt Modzelewski of Poland. This was put to a vote and defeated. Yugoslavia then proposed a second term for Lie. This was defeated by a single Russian veto vote, with Nationalist China abstaining to show its dislike for Lie. India proposed making up a list of twenty-two possible candidates. The permanent members would remove from the list those names unacceptable to them, and the election would be made—without veto—from those remaining. Russia readily agreed, for this would eliminate Lie from consideration. However, President Truman ordered Warren Austin, U.S. chief delegate at the time, to use the veto to prevent any action against Lie.

A United States veto would be just as binding on the Security Council as a Russian one. Malik gleefully used the situation for another attack on the United States and what he called "U.S. hypocrisy." In a speech to the Security Council, the Russian delegate said, "The United States, as a permanent member of the Security Council, has abandoned its widely advertised position of giving up the right of the veto. The United States representative [Warren Austin] has stated that he would veto any candidate other than Mr. Lie, and thus intends to promote Mr. Lie's candidacy, even though the latter is illegal, by resort to the veto."

The United States position was not so much due to regard for Lie as it was a fight over basic principles. This position was summed up by the Norwegian representative to the UN, who made a speech supporting his fellow countryman, Lie. He said that Russia was retaliating against Lie "because of his stand under the 99th Article of the Charter [Lie's action in calling the Security Council to consider the North Korean attack]. Mr. Lie's elimination would be tantamount to victory for the North Koreans."

It must be said here that Russian opposition to Lie was not just a matter of pique but represented a fundamental difference of policy between East and West. Under Lie the office of the Secretary-General had taken on increased importance. In view of this, both opposing sides wanted a man in office favorable to them.

Other names were proposed, including Sir Bengal Rau of India, Charles Malik of Lebanon, and Carlos Romulo of the Philippines. All were voted down, leaving the Security Council in a deadlock. The Council then voted, over Soviet objections, to inform the General Assembly that it was unable to agree on a nominee. Since this was a matter of procedure, the vote was not subject to Soviet veto. When the General Assembly received the notification of the Security Council deadlock, a fifteen-nation bloc introduced a joint resolution to extend Trygve Lie's term by three years. The argument was that the General Assembly could not elect a successor until a nomination was agreed on by the Security Council. Neither could the United Nations continue to function without a Secretary-General. Therefore, the Assembly had no alternative but to continue Lie in office. The United Nations Charter was specific in stating that the Secretary-General must have Security Council approval. However, this approval had been given when Lie was first elected in 1946. Despite the fight in the Security Council, the Council had not withdrawn this earlier approval since it was hopelessly deadlocked and could take no action pro or con on the question. Therefore, the Assembly considered itself legally competent to continue Lie in office.

By this time new admissions to the UN had increased membership to fifty-nine. In the showdown voting, Lie received forty-six votes to continue versus five votes from the Soviet bloc against the extension. In addition, there were eight abstainers. This included six members of the Arab bloc who resented what they considered Lie's favoritism to Israel; Australia, who questioned the legality of continuing Lie in office; and Nationalist China. The final vote was taken on October 1, 1951. Vyshinsky of Russia immediately announced that the Soviet bloc would not

This is where the United Nations Charter was born. W. L. Mackenzie King, chairman of the Canadian delegation, speaks at the second plenary session of the San Francisco conference in April 1945. The sessions were held in the War Memorial Opera House. UN PHOTO

Secretary of State Edward R. Stettinius, Jr., signs the UN Charter for the United States at the close of the San Francisco conference on June 26, 1945. President Harry S. Truman stands at the left. Members of the U.S. delegation to the conference stand at the right. UN PHOTO

The United Nations headquarters is spread through these buildings along New York City's East River. At right is the thirty-nine-story Secretariat Building; the Dag Hammarskjold Library is in the foreground, with the General Assembly Building behind the Secretariat. In the distance is the twin-spired Alcoa building, where UNICEF and the UN Development Program maintain offices. UN PHOTO

A battleground for peace is the UN Security Council, where some of the bitterest wars of words have been carried on. The chief delegates occupy chairs around the round table, with their advisers directly behind them. UN PHOTO

(Above) Korean refugees wait at a camp at Yongwol during the height of the fighting in Korea in 1951. U.S. ARMY PHOTO

(Below left) UN Secretary-General Dag Hammarskjöld arrives in Leopold-ville, Congo, on a peace mission and is greeted by Premier Cyrille Adoula, right, and Vice-Premier Antoine Gizenga (wearing glasses). UN PHOTO

(Below right) Soldiers from Egypt, Sweden and Ghana, symbolic of the multinational support of UN operations in the Congo, stand guard in Leopoldville. UN PHOTO

As in a scene from Beau Geste, *members of a Yugoslav unit of the United Nations Emergency Force patrol the sand dunes near El Arish in the Sinai Peninsula in January 1957.* UN PHOTO

A UN truce observation group in 1959 stops on a hill overlooking the Ain Sultain camp, which houses 17,500 Arab refugees from Palestine. The mounds of dirt at the right of the camp are excavations being carried out on the site of Jericho, the ancient biblical city. The Jordan River is in the background. UN PHOTO

Premier Khrushchev, acting as chairman of the Russian delegation during the historic fifteenth session of the General Assembly, rises to his feet to express his displeasure with a statement being made during an address of Prime Minister Harold Macmillan of Great Britain. Andrei Gromyko, USSR chief delegate to the UN, listens intently at left front. UN PHOTO

Dr. S. Jolibois of Haiti, a member of the UN's World Health Organization (WHO), vaccinates Congolese at Lisala on the Congo River during a 1963 epidemic of smallpox. UN PHOTO

(Above left) Dr. Gallego Garbayosa of Spain makes friends with a Burmese miss while checking children for leprosy as part of a combination WHO and UNICEF health program. UN PHOTO

(Above right) The UN Development Program provides expert advice and assistance to developing nations. Here a UN expert, left, works with a Bolivian in petroleum exploration in Bolivia. UN PHOTO

(Below) Two members of the UN Truce Supervision Organization stand watch from a UN post overlooking the Suez Canal in January 1969. On the left is an officer of the Irish Army, on the right an officer of the Swedish Air Force on duty at "Observation Post MIKE." UN PHOTO

The General Assembly meets in this dramatic setting in the United Nations Building in New York. The presiding officers sit on the high rostrum at the left under the United Nations emblem. This shows the opening of the twenty-sixth regular session in September 1971. UN PHOTO

Despite the heavy pressure of his duties as a keeper of the peace, Secretary-General Trygve Lie was always able to manage a broad smile. UN PHOTO

A smiling Red Chinese delegation is seated in the UN following the dramatic expulsion of the Nationalist Chinese delegation in 1971. In the left front row are Chiao Kuan-hua, delegation chairman; Huang Hua, vice-chairman; and Fu Hao, representative. UN PHOTO

The current Secretary-General Kurt Waldheim confers with Security Council President Omer Arteh Ghalib of Somalia during an unusual meeting of the Security Council in Addis Ababa, Ethiopia, in January 1972. Waldheim is the fourth man to hold the office of UN Secretary-General. UN PHOTO

recognize Lie as Secretary-General. For the remainder of his time in office, Russia completely ignored Lie and would conduct no business with the Secretary-General's office.

The vote extending Lie's term in office was taken just before China sent troops across the Yalu River to aid the North Koreans. The voting was done in an atmosphere of triumph, for those on the Western side believed MacArthur's claim that the war would be over by Christmas. The United States then decided that the time was ripe to push through a resolution called "Uniting for Peace." "Uniting for Peace" had been introduced by U.S. Secretary of State Dean Acheson in a September, 1950, speech. The plan was an attempt to find a means of skirting so many deadlocked Security Council meetings caused by the Russian veto. The plan, as introduced by Dean Acheson, called for:

•An emergency meeting of the General Assembly, to be called on twenty-four hours' notice, whenever the Security Council was prevented from acting because of a deadlock or otherwise.

•Establishment of a United Nations peace commission to provide immediate observations in situations where peace was threatened.

•Designation by each UN member of certain units of its armed forces to be made available for United Nations use in emergency and authorized interventions, such as Korea.

•Establishment of a special committee to work on plans for further collective action by the United Nations as a means of keeping the peace.

This proposal was aimed directly at Russia and the Russian veto which so often had deadlocked the Security Council. Even so, it was viewed with alarm by many Americans who saw in it a device under which a group of small nations could "gang up" on any of the Big Five, including the United States. In view of what was to happen twenty-one years later when the United States went down to a resounding defeat on the question of the admission of Red China, there was definite reason for such alarm.

As finally passed, the Uniting for Peace resolution provided that an emergency session of the General Assembly could be called "on the vote of any seven members of the Security Council." After the Security Council was enlarged, this was increased to a "vote of nine members." The final wording of the resolution reads:

> Resolved, that if the Security Council, because of lack of unanimity of the permanent members, fails to exercise its primary responsibility for the maintenance of international peace and security in any case where there appears to be a threat to the peace, breach of the peace, or act of aggression, the General Assembly shall consider the matter immediately with a view to making appropriate recommendations to Members for collective measures, including in the case of a breach of the peace or act of aggression the use of armed force when necessary. . . .

It should be borne in mind that this Uniting for Peace resolution uses the words "making appropriate *recommendations.*" Under the UN Charter only the Security Council can authorize the use of force to support any UN decision. This would appear to make the Uniting for Peace resolution nothing more than a means for the General Assembly to express its opinion. However, no nation was ordered to supply troops in the Korean War. The UN merely recommended that they do so, and sixteen responded.

In his autobiography Trygve Lie quotes a letter he received from General MacArthur at this time. MacArthur congratulated Lie on being extended in office and spoke of his delight in the passage of the Uniting for Peace resolution. "For your private consideration," MacArthur added, "it is my personal view . . . that you should now proceed vigorously to provide within the structure of the United Nations a permanent supreme military command . . . to effect the immediate deployment of the available military force to meet any emergency situation. . . ."

Lie adds that MacArthur in a later letter "offered his services as chief of such a permanent supreme military command. . . ."

Unfortunately for MacArthur's ambitions to step up from Supreme Commander of UN Forces in Korea to Supreme Commander of the United Nations Forces, his career as an active military commander was shortly to end. After being driven back to Wonsan by the entrance of the Chinese into the war, UN forces regained the initiative and slowly pushed the enemy back to a line just above the 38th parallel. Here things bogged down again. MacArthur, in his frustration at what he considered a continual political interference with his military objectives, wrote letters to members of the opposition Republican party in Congress. An angry President Truman then removed MacArthur from all military commands.

General MacArthur was relieved of his duty in April, 1951. During this time Trygve Lie was traveling in Europe and the Middle East. In his travels through Syria, Egypt, and Lebanon, Lie found that hatred of Israel was as great as ever, and the possibility of renewed fighting in Palestine seemed inevitable.

"There was hatred—bitter hatred," Lie wrote. "It was clear that the Arab states considered Israel a threat to their integrity and independence." In this respect, the Arabs' fanatical fear of Israel was caused both by their fury at Jewish occupation of what had been Arab territory and by uneasiness at the number of Jewish refugees who were pouring into Israel. In the Arab view, Israel would soon be overcrowded and would be seeking land in which to expand. She could only expand into neighboring Arab countries.

Lie also looked into the problem of Arab refugees from Palestine. At the time of the partition, 850,000 Arabs fled from their homes in the territory that became Israel and from areas involved in the subsequent fighting between Arabs and Jews. Jordan had 450,000 of these Arab refugees. There were another 130,000 in Egypt and Lebanon and 85,000 in Syria. None of these countries had facilities to care for so many homeless. The UN Relief and Work Agency was doing what it could to help, but the refugees were in a desperate situation.

Lie returned from his world trip to work actively toward restoring peace in Korea. The fighting had turned into a stalemate. Lie attempted to negotiate with a Peking delegation in December, 1951, but got nowhere. The Secretary-General now tried a different approach. In a speech delivered in Ottawa, Canada, Lie suggested that a fair end of the war could be negotiated by restoring the 38th parallel boundary between North and South Korea. Then Lie circulated a memorandum among UN delegates on their view of leaving cease-fire negotiations to the military commanders in the field. Lie had reason to believe that both Russia and China wanted to end the fighting. However, both nations had always insisted that any of their nationals who might be fighting in Korea were entirely volunteers. Therefore neither China nor Russia felt they could take direct action in the negotiations. Under

Lie's suggestion (later adopted by the U.S. State Department as the American position as well), the military commanders could negotiate a cease-fire between themselves but would discuss nothing of a political nature. This, in effect, would simply restore the 38th parallel border, since the fighting line approximated it anyway.

While Dean Acheson in his memoirs implies that the work of bringing about the cease-fire was entirely the work of his State Department, it seems clear from other accounts that the bulk of the negotiations and planning was done by the UN Secretary-General. Lie had arranged for a series of radio talks by prominent UN officials on the subject of "The Price of Peace." On one of these Yakov Malik said, "The Soviet people believe the first step [toward peace in Korea] would be discussions toward a cease-fire."

Lie, as a means of putting more pressure on North Korea and Red China, announced that he was prepared to make another world trip to convince governments of the United Nations that they should allot more troops to the fighting in Korea. After the United States ambassador to Russia reported that the Russian government was sincere in its call for a cease-fire, General Matthew B. Ridgway, who had succeeded MacArthur as UN commander in Korea, broadcast a statement to the Commander, Communist Forces in Korea, suggesting that the military commanders send representatives to discuss a cease-fire. Kaesong, a Korean town between the fighting lines, was agreed on as the negotiation site.

The negotiations turned out to be a continual fight between the United States and the Communists over the line of demarcation between North and South Korea. Negotiations were broken off and later resumed at Panmunjon, near Kaesong, following bitter fighting that resulted in new UN victories. After more delays caused by disagreements over prisoner-of-war repatriation, the cease-fire was signed in July, 1953.

During the final months of the fighting in Korea, while definite steps were being made toward peace, the office of the Secretary-General of the United Nations was involved in a bitter war of its own. Although Lie was being boycotted by the Russians for being a "tool of the West," he now came under a particularly vicious attack by anti-Communist forces in the United States who accused him of packing the secretariat with Communists.

At this time Senator Joseph McCarthy of Wisconsin was leading a fight against what he called Communist influences in the United States government. McCarthyism, as his methods were called, reached proportions of hysteria, and many innocent persons came under attack. After American Communists—the Rosenbergs—were accused of passing secrets about the atom bomb to Russia, and a State Department employee, Judith Coplan, was convicted of passing U.S. secrets to Valentin Gubitchev, a Russian employed in the UN secretariat, the anti-Communist forces had solid material to support their claims of Communist infiltration. Then Alger Hiss, a former State Department official who had been instrumental in the formation of the United Nations, was accused of spying for Russia. All this created American public support for McCarthyism.

The trouble for Lie was compounded in October, 1952, when the U.S. Senate's Internal Security Subcommittee held public hearings in New York. Eighteen American employees of the United Nations, asked about their Communist ties, pleaded the Fifth Amendment on the grounds that their answers would incriminate them.

Lie wrote later, "Although these witnesses were about

one in a hundred of the Americans employed by the United Nations, the impression conveyed to the public was that of a parade of Americans working for the United Nations who were Communists, former Communists, or at least had something to hide."

There was tremendous pressure on Lie to dismiss those American employees of the UN who refused to testify. A New York grand jury, although it failed to return any indictments, rendered a report claiming the UN secretariat was riddled with Soviet spies. Lie, who certainly had an anti-Communist background, tried to form a committee of famous judges to give him an opinion, but a surprising number of top jurists refused to serve. He finally persuaded three to serve. They were Will D. Mitchell, a former U.S. attorney general; Sir Edwin Hubert of Great Britain; and Paul Veldekens, law professor at the Catholic University, Louvain, Belgium.

The group ruled that inasmuch as the UN secretariat staff regulations read: " . . . Members of the Secretariat . . . shall avoid any actions and in particular any kind of public pronouncements which may adversely reflect on their status . . . ," then Lie was legally authorized to dismiss those who took the Fifth Amendment and refused to testify as to their present or past affiliation with Communist groups. This course was the one Lie followed.

This was a period of great bitterness for the embattled Secretary-General. The condemnation following the Communist "witch hunting," as McCarthy's enemies termed it, coming on top of Lie's difficulties with the Russian boycott of his office, sickened the Norwegian to the point where he decided to resign.

Lie found only one cheerful thing in his job at this time. The United Nations finally moved into its permanent headquarters in downtown New York. Some of the staff and agencies had moved in earlier, but the September, 1952, meeting of the General Assembly was the first in the new buildings.

After John D. Rockefeller, Jr., gave $8,500,000 to buy the land, the United States advanced the UN a loan of $65 million dollars to get the building construction underway. The loan was interest-free and was to be repaid over a period of thirty years. Inflation added an extra two million to the construction cost before the headquarters complex was finished.

Trygve Lie laid the cornerstone for the headquarters building on United Nations Day, October 24, 1946, sealing inside a copy of the UN Charter and a copy of the Universal Declaration of Human Rights. The original plan called for a thirty-nine-story secretariat building and two long, lower structures for a conference building and the General Assembly building. The secretariat building was completed first, and the first personnel moved into it in late 1950. The building was faced with aluminum and blue-green glass with gray marble on the ends. The conference building, which houses several special agencies, lies alongside New York's East River. It is a four-story building created from limestone and glass. The General Assembly building was built last. Inside, its main lobby is opened to a domed roof. A ramp leads to the delegates' auditorium, and there is a visitors' gallery.

The General Assembly auditorium is half the size of a football field and is covered by a high vaulted ceiling pierced by a skylight. There is a rostrum for speakers and the Assembly president and Secretary-General. The delegates have curved rows of wooden desks facing the rostrum. Interpreters have rooms in glass-enclosed tiers along the side walls. When a delegate speaks, these interpreters simultaneously translate his words into the official

UN languages: English, Chinese, French, Russian, and Spanish. The translations are carried by wires to the desk of each delegate. The delegate has a set of earphones connected to a dial with six numbers. Dial number one transmits the voice of the speaker in the language that he is using. The remaining five dials are set up to carry a translation in each of the five official languages. In order to follow the discussions, the delegates must know one of the official languages.

When the General Assembly opened its session in the new building in September, 1952, Trygve Lie had already made his decision to resign, but he did not make his announcement until November 10. He had hoped to end his duties by the close of November, but a fight developed in the Security Council over the choice of a successor. Lie remained on the job until one was named.

Carlos Romulo of the Philippines, Ambassador Valerian Zorin of the U.S.S.R., and Foreign Minister Stanislaw Skrzeszewski of Poland were nominated and defeated by vetoes. Lester B. Pearson of Canada received nine votes but was stopped by a Russian veto.

The Big Five holders of the veto met together, seeking some compromise candidate on whom they could all agree. Dozens of names were considered, including Prince Wan Waithayakon of Thailand, Charles Malik of Lebanon, Benegal Rau of India, Henri Spaak of Belgium, Ahmed Bokhari of Pakistan, and Eduardo Zuleta Angel of Colombia. None was acceptable to one side or the other. Three months had passed since Lie had tendered his resignation. Vyshinsky became alarmed at the failure to agree. Lie had agreed to remain in office until a successor was named. Continual disagreement could mean that Lie would become the permanent "temporary" Secretary-General. The West equally realized that continual disagreement was fatal to the future of the United Nations. Work of the UN had been hamstrung for three years by Russia's boycott of the Secretary-General's office. New problems were looming on the international horizon, and a unified effort behind a new Secretary-General was essential.

Finally, on March 31, the Big Five agreed on a dark horse candidate whose nomination surprised the General Assembly. The selectee was Dag Hammarskjöld, a minister in the Swedish government. Hammarskjöld was as surprised as anyone else but accepted the nomination and the position when it was confirmed by the General Assembly on April 7, 1953. Along with the title of Secretary-General of the United Nations, Hammarskjöld also received this prophetic admonition from Trygve Lie: "The task of Secretary-General is the most impossible job on earth."

CHAPTER 9

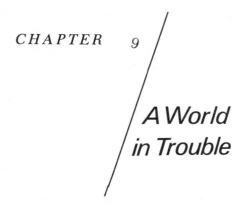

A World in Trouble

Trygve Lie had increased the stature of the office of Secretary-General far beyond what the drafters of the UN Charter had intended. His successor, Dag Hammarskjöld, in time would go beyond Lie in increasing the importance of the position.

Major General Carl Von Horn, who commanded UN forces in Palestine and the Congo, described Hammarskjöld in this manner:

> He was just as I remembered him, of medium stature, fair haired, brisk and alert in an outwardly rather cool impersonal way. . . . There was something dedicated about him, perhaps some powerful inner ambition closely intermingled with idealism.

The new Secretary-General quickly showed that he had great faith in the United Nations but little faith in the United Nations' processes and ways of doing things. Instead of relying on fruitless debate in the Security Council and the General Assembly, Hammarskjöld preferred to handle matters through personal contact and diplomacy.

As a result, he traveled more than Lie, visiting countries and scenes of international disturbances. More and more problems were thrashed out in conferences in his office and in the offices of various delegates. As time went on, it became increasingly popular for delegates to wash their hands of problems by saying, "Let Dag do it." In many cases Dag "did it," but the international problems were so tremendous and national interests so stubborn that he had many failures.

Hammarskjöld's administration started well. Two months after he assumed office the Korean War armistice was signed. The General Assembly was able to report that colonialism was rapidly disappearing. When the United Nations was formed, there were 800 million people under colonial governments. This number had now been cut to 200 million. The other 600 million were now under independent national governments, many of whom had become members of the United Nations. Then on December 8, 1953, President Dwight D. Eisenhower proposed an "Atoms for Peace" plan to the eighth session of the General Assembly. The plan was in answer to a resolution passed in September in which the General Assembly called on the nuclear powers to seek among themselves a disarmament plan to avoid a nuclear armament race which, the Assembly said, "overshadows not only peace but the very life of the world." In his reply, Eisenhower said, "It is not enough to take this weapon out of the hands of the soldiers. It must be put in the hands of those who will know how to strip its [the atom bomb's] military casing and adapt it to the arts of peace."

While these worthwhile accomplishments were being made, the world was slowly moving toward new crises. The cold war between the Communists and the West was dormant from 1953 to 1956, and Dag Hammarskjöld's "personal diplomacy" received much of the credit for this. But if the big powers were striving to be peaceful, the same cannot be said of the smaller nations. Indochina was in a struggle for independence from France. Indonesia was trying to oust the Netherlands from the last of her possessions in Asia. India and Pakistan were still quarreling over Kashmir, and Algeria also sought independence.

Under the UN Charter the United Nations is restricted to international disputes. Internal disorders are beyond the scope of the Security Council unless the UN is asked to intervene by the legal government of the country involved. However, in 1955, the French colonies in North Africa were agitating for independence. This had been promised, but little was being done about it. The Arab bloc introduced a resolution in the General Assembly for a debate on the subject. France angrily retorted that this was an internal matter beyond the scope of the United Nations Charter. The Arab bloc, supported by the large number of small nations who had been admitted to the UN, mustered sufficient votes to put the question on the agenda anyway. The French delegation then walked out, to the consternation of the small nations who had voted for the Arab resolution.

These small nations saw the United Nations as their only bulwark against aggression from their neighbors and the larger nations. France's withdrawal, following as it did Russia's long boycott during the final three years of Trygve Lie's administration, gave warning that the UN was in danger of dissolving. There were hurried attempts to placate France. The French delegates returned to the Assembly, and the North African debate was quietly dropped.

This in itself was a small matter, but the implications were much greater. It showed the rising power of the small nations in the UN and the force of their combined vote. In the General Assembly a nation of 200 million people has one vote. Maldive, a nation of only 100,000 people, also has one vote. It was to protect the big nations from a "gang-up" by groups of smaller nations that the veto in the Security Council was conceived. In this case, regardless of the rights or wrongs of French treatment of Arab colonials in North Africa, the matter was an internal French problem and, by the UN Charter, outside the responsibility of the UN.

Two major events of 1955 were Dag Hammarskjöld's trip to Red China where he negotiated the release of a United States air crew who had been shot down over North Korea, and a compromise on admission of a group of new countries to the United Nations. For several years no new nations had been admitted because of a disagreement between East and West. The United States and her allies objected to the admission of Albania, Bulgaria, Hungary, and Rumania because of their support of Germany in World War II. Russia in turn was adamant against the admission of Ireland, Spain, and Japan, among others.

In December, 1955, Canada offered a resolution that included all eighteen of the disputed countries in a "package deal" that gave each side what it wanted in exchange for compromising on what the other side desired. The countries included were Albania, Austria, Bulgaria, Cambodia, Ceylon, Finland, Hungary, Ireland, Italy, Japan, Jordan, Laos, Libya, Nepal, Outer Mongolia, Portugal, Rumania, and Spain. The resolution passed the Assembly and was sent to the Security Council, which is required to pass on all admissions to the UN. Nationalist China was adamantly against admission of Outer Mongolia, which the Chinese delegate characterized as a Russian puppet. Russia's representative, Arkady Sobolev, insisted that the

Council had to accept the total package of eighteen countries or none. China threatened to veto the proposal, but before a vote could be taken, the International Court of Justice ruled that the UN Charter did not provide for mass admissions and that each name on the list would have to be considered individually.

When the vote was taken on each nation under consideration, Russia vetoed all except those of the Russian bloc, and Nationalist China vetoed Outer Mongolia. It seemed then that all eighteen would be excluded. However, several days later Sobolev returned with a new proposal, which in effect was another package deal. He would bow to the Outer Mongolian veto, "even though it was cast by a person illegally holding the seat rightfully belonging to Communist China." In exchange for excluding Outer Mongolia, he demanded the exclusion of Japan. He would then withdraw the Soviet vetoes on the remaining nations. This was agreed, and the other sixteen nations were admitted to the United Nations.

Japan was admitted the following year, after Russia and the Japanese signed a treaty. Russian objection to Japan's entrance into the UN in 1955 and the about-face in 1956 were due to international politics. The reversal helped save face over the rejection of Outer Mongolia. It also gave Russia a bargaining point in the treaty talks with Japan. In addition, it served notice on Japan that she could not continue to depend on the United States but would have to consider Russia in her future international intercourse. It had become a favorite Russian diplomatic ploy to use her UN vote and veto for political purposes even when the question involved was of little intrinsic interest to her. For example, twice Russia vetoed questions of interest to Indonesia, not because they meant anything to Russia, but in order to show friendship for Indonesia.

Another question of importance that came up at this tenth session of the United Nations was whether the Charter should be amended. This was provided for in the Charter, and the ten-year milestone seemed a good time to assess the UN's accomplishments and shortcomings during its first years of operation. The question was placed on the agenda over Soviet opposition, but a series of conferences showed that it would be impossible to amend the Charter at this time. The differences between the big powers were too great to arrive at any possible chance of agreement. The smaller nations were pushing for removal of the veto, but all of the Big Five were united in rejecting this change. Russia was using the veto as a matter of policy. While decrying Russia's use of the veto, the United States had threatened to use it herself in the fight over Trygve Lie's extension of office. Great Britain and France were preparing to use it in a new crisis that was building up in the Middle East. China had vetoed the admission of Outer Mongolia.

In the end, the consensus of opinion was that amendment of the UN Charter should wait for a better time. As it happened, the world's nations were in closer agreement in 1955 than they would be again. The following year brought two major crises—one of which took the world to the brink of war and was one of the greatest crises in the entire history of the United Nations. This was the Suez problem, which eventually involved Egypt, Israel, France, and England in armed hostilities.

President Gamal Abdel Nasser of Egypt triggered the crisis, but it was actually a product of World War I. In the sixteenth century the Middle East was overrun by the Ottoman Turks, who ruled over the Arabs for the next 400 years. During World War I the Turks declared for Germany, setting the stage for invasion of Palestine and surrounding areas by British forces from Egypt. Great Britain was extremely anxious to obtain control of Palestine, Iraq, and the Sinai Peninsula because of their proximity to the Suez Canal. The canal was Great Britain's lifeline to trade in India and the Orient. If the canal fell into unfriendly hands, it would force shipping between the Orient and England to circle the tip of Africa, almost doubling the cost of transportation.

The Suez Canal links the Mediterranean Sea with the Gulf of Aqaba and the Red Sea. It was dug under the direction of the Frenchman Ferdinand de Lesseps between 1859 and 1869. It was cut through a strip of Egyptian territory leased from the Khedive of Egypt for ninety-nine years. Under terms of the lease, the entire canal would become Egyptian property at the expiration of the lease in 1968. Until then, it would be operated by the Suez Canal Company. The company's stock was jointly owned by French capitalists and the Khedive of Egypt.

Great Britain was worried about France, a traditional enemy, controlling the canal but in 1875 was able to buy the shares controlled by the Khedive of Egypt who was near bankruptcy. The canal was then operated by French and British interests with no profit to the Egyptian government. At that time the British moved troops into Egypt to protect their interest in the Canal, and the troops remained until 1955. An Egyptian revolt in 1952 had overthrown King Farouk and in 1954 brought Nasser to power in the country. Nasser faced overwhelming problems. Fighting was going on along the Israeli border. Thirteen thousand Arab refugees from Palestine were screaming for war with Israel. And the majority of his people were ragged and hungry.

Nasser's solution to the hunger problem was a plan to build a new dam at Aswan on the Nile which would provide both electric power for new industries and additional water for irrigation so that the narrow strip of cultivated area along the Nile could be increased. The United States, Great Britain, and the World Bank agreed to fund the project, but the United States withdrew in early 1956. Nasser's recognition of Red China and rapport with Russia were given as the reasons. The announcement of U.S. withdrawal, which was followed shortly by the withdrawal of Great Britain and the World Bank, was made on July 22, 1956. Three days later a furious Nasser told his people in a rousing speech that he was nationalizing the Suez Canal and would use the canal fees to build the Aswan Dam. Under the original lease Egypt would have been given the canal in another twelve years. Nasser needed something to bolster himself after losing out on the original Aswan Dam plan and took this means of doing it.

The expropriation of the canal caused consternation in Europe, for the Suez Canal was vital to European trade. As a result representatives from twenty-four nations formed a Canal Users' Association, demanding that the canal be placed under international control. Nasser angrily refused. In a fiery speech in Cairo, the Egyptian president cried, "The Suez Canal has become our property and the Egyptian flag flies over it. We shall hold it with our blood, and we shall meet aggression with agression and evil with evil. We shall proceed toward achieving dignity with prestige for Egypt!"

Christian Pineau, premier of France, was under pressure from French investors in the canal, and Great Britain was concerned about losing her trade routes. In September, 1956, both nations referred the Suez problem to the Security Council, and it came up for debate in October. The Egyptian UN delegate denounced France and Great

Britain. He was supported by a Russian veto of a proposed resolution.

To everyone's surprise, Nasser ran the canal efficiently. However, he ordered the waterway closed to Israeli ships. The resulting loss of trade put Israel in a desperate situation. Palestine had always been a poor country. While Jewish industry and exceptionally hard work had made their nation far more productive than it had been under the Arabs, Israel was surviving only because of foreign aid and monetary support from Zionists around the world. An appreciable trade loss, such as the Suez Canal restriction caused, was a disaster. At the same time Israel had to fight guerrilla bands of Arabs all along her frontier.

At this point it may seem that the Arabs had been the villains in the Middle East story. However, it must be remembered that during World War I, when the Balfour Declaration was issued promising the establishment of a Jewish national homeland in Palestine, Arabs had been fighting with the British to free Palestine from the Turks. To the Arabs, the creation of Israel by the UN in 1947 had been a betrayal. Actually it would have been more just if their anger had been directed toward Great Britain instead of Israel, for the cause of all the trouble originated in London. The Israelis were a harassed, homeless people who were trying for the first time in centuries to put roots down in what they could call their own native land.

Israel now felt that her entire future depended on immediate action. Consequently, the Israeli army launched a sudden attack on Egypt, driving deeply into the Sinai Peninsula. The result was startling. Egypt had been stockpiling huge amounts of Russian-supplied weapons, while Israel had had her arms shipments cut by the United States as a measure to prevent war in the Middle East. Despite the tremendous material advantage Egypt had, the better-trained and better-led Israeli army smashed through the Egyptian defenses. Within three days the Israelis had crossed the Sinai Peninsula and were nearing the banks of the Suez Canal.

Britain and France issued a demand to both Israel and Egypt to stop fighting, threatening to send their own troops in to protect the canal. Their ultimatum threw President Eisenhower into a fury. Neither France nor England had consulted the United States before issuing their threat to intervene in the Israeli–Egyptian war. Eisenhower felt that their actions could well trigger another world war. He demanded that Henry Cabot Lodge, the U.S. chief delegate to the UN, introduce a resolution in the Security Council ordering an immediate cease-fire. The American president bluntly accused Britain, Israel, and France of violating the UN Charter. France and Britain promptly vetoed the resolution.

The stated purpose of Britain and France's threatened intervention in the fighting was to protect the Suez Canal and restore order. A UN-sponsored cease-fire would have accomplished these aims. Yet both countries used the veto—which they had criticized Russia for using—to prevent a UN order for a cease-fire. This action gave support to those who claimed that Israel attacked Egypt only because of a secret agreement whereby France and England would support the Israelis in exchange for the return of the Suez Canal when Nasser was defeated.

At the same time as the trouble over the Suez Canal, a revolt erupted in Hungary. In October, 1956, students and working men in Budapest, the capital, began demonstrations against the oppressive Hungarian Communist party of Erno Gero. The trouble spread, and Gero, in danger of seeing his regime collapse, frantically called on Russia for help. Russian occupation troops in Hungary immediately came to Gero's assistance. The movement of Russian troops triggered a full-scale battle with Hungarian Freedom Fighters. The death toll reached 23,000, with 200,000 refugees streaming into adjacent countries. The Hungarian premier, Janos Kadar, in reply to a General Assembly resolution, said that Russian troops were in Hungary at his request and that there was nothing to warrant UN observers. Hammarskjöld then asked to be permitted to come to Budapest himself. He was told that he would be welcome as a tourist but not as the Secretary-General of the United Nations.

Russia, in turn, let it be known that any attempt to help the Hungarian Freedom Fighters was an act of war against the Soviet Union. In these circumstances, the UN was powerless. Absolutely nothing could be done short of war between Russia and the United States. The United States, through its UN chief delegate, Henry Cabot Lodge, continued to denounce Russian activity in suppressing the Hungarian revolt, but everyone understood that this was solely for its propaganda effect. The United States had no intention of going to war with Russia over the Hungarian problem.

The Russian army restored order in the country by November 8, 1956, and the Security Council went back to considering the far more explosive question of the Suez Canal. Hammarskjöld, however, was not one to take a defeat lightly. He knew that it was impossible for the UN to act effectively against either of the superpowers. He did, however, realize the propaganda value of the Hungarian situation as a weapon against Russia. He persuaded the General Assembly to establish a special committee to interview Hungarian refugees and determine just what happened in Hungary at the time of the Russian intervention.

The resulting report, issued in June, 1957, was harshly denounced by Russia's Arkady Sobolev, who accused Hammarskjöld of using the office of Secretary-General to spread capitalist propaganda. Curiously enough, this attack did not affect Russia's attitude toward Hammarskjöld's reelection as Secretary-General. The implication here is that Nikita Khrushchev, the Russian premier, was not averse to having the situation in Hungary revealed. The stories told by the refugees were sufficiently shocking to deter similar revolts in other Soviet satellites.

Hammarskjöld's term of office expired in the spring of 1958, and his reelection was considered at the opening session of the UN in September, 1957. He received the Russian vote in the Security Council and was elected by the General Assembly. In his acceptance speech on September 26, 1957, the Secretary-General took the occasion to reaffirm his views of the office.

In the multidimensional world of diplomacy, the Euclidean definition of the straight line as the shortest way between two points may not always hold true. For the Secretary-General, however, it is the only possible one. This line, as traced by the principles which are the law for him, might at times cross other lines in the intricate pattern of international political action. He must then be able to feel secure that, whatever the difficulties, they will not impair the trust of Member governments to his Office.

I do not believe that the Secretary-General should be asked to act, by the Member States, if no guidance for his action is to be found either in the Charter or in the decisions of the main organs of the United Nations; within the limits thus set, however, I believe it to be his duty to use his office and, indeed, the machinery of the Organization to its utmost capacity and to the full extent permitted at each stage by practical circumstances.

On the other hand, I believe that it is in keeping with the philosophy of the Charter that the Secretary-General should be expected to act also without such guidance, should this appear to him necessary in order to help in filling any vacuum that may appear in the systems which the Charter and traditional diplomacy provide for safeguarding peace and security.

Here Hammarskjöld was bluntly warning the Assembly that if it could not or would not give him the guidance and support he needed in fighting for peace, he had the authority under the UN Charter to take action on his own initiative. As to whether this action would be successful or not, he said:

The many who, together, form this Organization—peoples, governments and individuals—share one great responsibility. Future generations may come to say of us that we never achieved what we set out to do. May they never be entitled to say that we failed because we lacked faith or permitted narrow self-interest to distort our efforts.

These words were prophetic. Within four years Dag Hammarskjöld would be dead—killed in the performance of UN duties. He died without achieving what he set out to do, but there is none who can say that he lacked faith in what he strived to accomplish or that he let narrow self-interest distort his efforts.

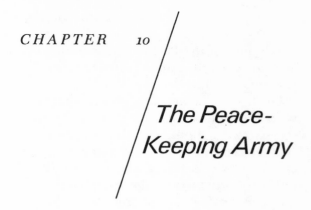

CHAPTER   10

*The Peace-
Keeping Army*

As the Hungarian crisis faded, the situation in the Middle East grew worse. Great Britain and France were determined to destroy Nasser. They vetoed the Security Council's cease-fire resolution, while Russia warned that if the war continued the Arabs would "not stand alone." On October 30, French troop transports sailed from Marseilles, and British transports put out from the island of Malta. The next day British Royal Air Force planes from Cyprus bombed Egyptian airfields in preparation for the troop landings.

The soldiers were headed for Suez. Nasser retaliated by sinking some Egyptian ships to block the canal. Syrian terrorists, sympathizing with Nasser, blew up the oil pipelines that supplied Europeans with oil from Iraq. What France and Britain feared would happen was now a reality. The only way Arabian oil could reach Europe was in tankers sailing around the tip of Africa. Not only did this greatly increase the transportation route and costs, but there were not enough tankers to meet the supply demands.

The Security Council was paralyzed by the combined vetoes of France and Great Britain. The United States opposed Israel, France, and Great Britain. John Foster Dulles, the U.S. secretary of state, told the General Assembly on November 1, ". . .the United States finds itself unable to agree with three nations with whom it has ties, deep friendship, admiration and respect, and two of whom [France and Great Britain] constitute our oldest, most trusted and reliable allies."

With the Security Council unable to act, the problem was referred to the General Assembly under the "Uniting for Peace" resolution. It was well past midnight on November 2, 1956, when the exhausted delegates finally got around to voting on the cease-fire resolution. Sixty-four nations voted for it. Great Britain, France, Israel, Australia, and New Zealand voted against; Belgium, Canada, Laos, the Netherlands, Portugal, and South Africa abstained. There were then seventy-five members in the General Assembly.

The UN cease-fire vote did not end the hostilities. The "Uniting for Peace" resolution under which the Assembly acted is not binding. The General Assembly can recommend and "call upon" nations to act, but it is powerless to order. Only the Security Council can give orders that can be backed up with force. Since the United Nations could not use force, Russia threatened to permit "volunteers" to join in the fighting unless an immediate cease-fire was put into effect. This threat was issued on November 4, two days after the first UN cease-fire resolution was passed.

Israel's reply to the cease-fire resolution was a refusal to retreat from land she had gained in the Sinai Peninsula unless the UN guaranteed Israeli borders and provided means of stopping Arab attacks along the Israeli frontiers.

Both Britain and France insisted on remaining in the Suez area until some international force capable of keeping order could take control.

Lester B. Pearson of Canada, a man many thought should have been elected Secretary-General instead of either Trygve Lie or Dag Hammarskjöld, then proposed such an international force acting under UN orders, but composed of French and British soldiers. Dag Hammarskjöld objected to the inclusion of these two countries. He felt there would be greater acceptance of a UN force to oversee peace in the Middle East if members of the supervisory force were from the small nations. Pearson introduced the resolution in a night meeting on November 4 to set up a United Nations Emergency Force to "secure and supervise the cessation of hostilities in the Middle East."

Formation of the UNEF was left to Hammarskjöld, who ignored the Military Staff Committee of the Security Council because it was composed of members from the five permanent members. Instead he drew the Emergency Force from India, Denmark, Norway, Sweden, Colombia, Finland, Indonesia, Yugoslavia, and Canada. Command of the UNEF international army was given to Major General E. L. M. Burns of Canada.

The resolution to form the UNEF was passed by the General Assembly on November 4, and by November 15 the first troops were flown to Egypt aboard Swissair planes. The soldiers wore their national uniforms, modified with U.S. army helmets painted sky blue, with blue United Nations Emergency Force armbands.

It is important to remember that the UNEF was not sent to the Middle East to fight. Punitive action was entirely the prerogative of the Security Council. UNEF was intended to act as a buffer between the Israeli and Egyptian (Arab) forces. The theory was that neither side would attack the United Nations, and if the United Nations was between the two, there could be no resumption of the fighting. General Burns was supposed to oversee the cease-fire and the withdrawal of British and French troops and to care for refugees.

Israel pulled back from the Sinai Peninsula but was bitter toward Hammarskjöld, whom she blamed for saving Nasser. Later when the Secretary-General visited Israel, he was met by demonstrators who carried placards calling him "Nassershield." The term was a pun on his own name which translates as "Hammer Shield," a name conferred on a warrior ancestor by King Charles II in 1611. It is also said that Golda Meir, then Israeli foreign minister, drew on her previous experience as a schoolteacher in Milwaukee, Wisconsin, to lecture Dag as if he were a schoolboy. It was plain to all that the Palestine question was not settled. Everyone wondered when it would explode again, and where.

The truce in the Suez war was followed by a steady stream of troubles around the world. Syria claimed she was being threatened by concentrations of Turkish troops along her northern border. Lebanon and Jordan complained that the United Arab Republic was meddling in their internal affairs. The quarrel over the island of Cyprus (between Greece and Great Britain) was again noted by the Security Council. Russia complained that flights of the United States Strategic Air Command bombers, armed with nuclear weapons, constituted a threat to international security. The question of *apartheid*—separation of races—in South Africa was brought up for about the fourth time.

A completely different type of complaint came in June, 1960. A Jewish group dedicated to finding Nazi war criminals located fugitive Adolf Eichmann in Argentina. Eichmann, a high Nazi official under Adolf Hitler, was charged with murdering a large number of Jewish prisoners during the Nazi reign. Eichmann was spirited out of Argentina and taken to Israel for trial. Argentina brought the matter to the notice of the Security Council, charging "the violation of the sovereign rights of the Argentine Republic resulting from the illicit and clandestine transfer of Adolf Eichmann . . . to Israel."

The Council debated the complaint on June 22. Golda Meir was invited to attend without vote. Mrs. Meir acknowledged that "the persons" who spirited Eichmann out of Argentina broke that republic's laws, and offered Israel's apology. However, she added that "the exceptional and unique character of the crimes [genocide] attributed to Eichmann" should be considered. The Council voted to adopt the Argentine resolution, which emphasized the necessity of safeguarding the sovereign rights of states and called on Israel to pay reparations to Argentina. Mrs. Meir then said that her government considered that its expression of regret was adequate reparation.

All of these problems and crises were dwarfed by the explosion that broke out in the Congo in 1960. In the beginning the UN and Dag Hammarskjöld tried to handle the crises the same way they had successfully met the challenge of war in the Middle East. Unfortunately, no two problems can be solved with the same answer, and the UN found itself involved in an actual shooting war for the first time since the Korean tragedy.

The Congo crisis officially began for the United Nations on July 14, 1960, when the Security Council adopted a resolution ordering Belgium to withdraw her troops from the Congo and authorizing Hammarskjöld to provide the Congo with military and technical assistance until this new nation was able to take care of herself. However, the problem really began in 1878 when King Leopold II of Belgium commissioned Henry M. Stanley to establish trading stations along the Congo River in central Africa. (Stanley is best remembered today for finding the lost missionary, Dr. Livingstone, in Africa.)

In 1885 thirteen European nations signed the Berlin treaty, which permitted King Leopold to form the Congo Free State. This was a curious arrangement. The Free State was not a Belgian colony but the private domain of the king. A paper prepared for the Dag Hammarskjöld forum by members of the Association of the Bar of the City of New York referred to the Free State as "a corporate estate with a monarch as the squire."

The Congo is rich in mineral wealth. Its mines, together with the growing importance of its rubber plantations, produced tremendous profits at the expense of actual slavery for the native Congolese. The forced labor scandals became so great that the Free State was changed to a Belgian colony in 1908. Things improved gradually after this. After World War II brought wide reaction against colonialism and an increasing agitation for independence, Belgium began making drastic and almost revolutionary changes in her handling of the Congo. More profits from the mines were plowed back into public programs, and laws were passed to eliminate segregation. By 1955 foreign observers considered the Congo a model colony. But despite their liberalism in many aspects, the Belgians were careful to exclude the Congolese from any important government and civil service positions. Nor could a native expect to rise higher than warrant officer in the *Force Publique* (army). In addition, there was a subdued, but vicious, hatred of Europeans seething under the calm surface of the colony.

Agitation for independence ballooned between 1955

and 1960, fostered by two rival politicians, Joseph Kasavubu and Patrice Lumumba. This agitation led to a declaration of independence by the Congo on June 30, 1960. The country was not ready for political freedom, but Belgium had to agree to the independence move or fight a costly, bloody war. With anticolonialism sweeping the world, the Belgians could expect nothing but censure and trouble if they chose to fight for their African colony. On the other hand, if they gave independence to the Congo, they hoped to hold their economic position in Central Africa. The Congolese were not able to run the mines and plantations, conduct the government, or staff the *Force Publique*. Because these managerial positions had always been filled by Belgians, no Congolese had been trained to take their places. The Belgians believed that at least 50,-000 of the 115,000 Europeans in the Belgian Congo would be required to keep the country afloat after independence.

They were correct in believing the Congolese could not manage their country, but incorrect in assuming that the natives would tolerate Belgians in their country any longer. Trouble erupted as soon as the Belgian flag was lowered over the government buildings in Leopoldville, the capital of Belgian Congo. Kasavubu and Lumumba temporarily shelved their differences in the interest of getting the Belgians out of the Congo. Kasavubu was president of the new republic, and Lumumba became prime minister. Neither was able to control the *Force Publique* when it turned on its white officers. Then hate-motivated citizens began to attack their former masters. Lumumba put the army under two former sergeants, Victor Lundula and Joseph Mobutu, who did nothing to halt the growing anarchy. Hordes of panic-stricken Europeans (and some Americans) fled the city as murder, rape, and pillage increased.

The Belgian government began flying troops back to the Congo on July 8. Three days later Lumumba sent a frantic wire asking the United States to send troops to the Congo to oust the Belgians. President Eisenhower refused Lumumba's plea for U.S. Marines to back his authority against the Belgians. On the same day Moise Tshombe, a tribal leader in the Congo's Katanga province, announced the secession of Katanga from the Congo. Katanga held most of the Congo's mineral wealth. The secession, if successful, would be a disaster to the faltering Congolese government.

Lumumba and Kasavubu then called on the United Nations. Dag Hammarskjöld called an emergency meeting of the Security Council on July 13. A bitter fight erupted among the delegates, but the Council finally agreed on a resolution at 4:00 A.M. on July 14. The resolution—which itself would spark greater trouble later— read:

> Considering the request for military assistance addressed to the Secretary-General by the President and the Prime Minister of the Republic of the Congo,
>
> 1. [The Security Council] calls upon the Government of Belgium to withdraw their troops from the territory of the Republic of the Congo;
>
> 2. Decides to authorize the Secretary-General to take the necessary steps, in consultation with the Government of the Congo, to provide the Government with military assistance as may be necessary. . . .

Once again the Security Council took the easy way out by "shoving it up to the 38th floor." The thirty-eighth floor housed Hammarskjöld's offices. The Secretary-General's solution to the problem was to organize another UN emergency force like the one which had been so successful in providing a buffer between the Egyptians and Israelis in the Holy Land. This one was called ONUC (for the French *Operation des Nations Unies au Congo*). Once again Hammarskjöld excluded the big powers and called on smaller nations to furnish troops. The ONUC was under the direct supervision of the Secretary-General. He gave its commander specific orders to use force only in self-defense and not to intervene in the internal affairs of the Republic of the Congo. They were there solely to restore order.

The first ONUC troops into the Congo were from Ghana. On their arrival, fighting stopped between the Belgians and the Congolese, but Tshombe in Katanga refused to permit ONUC forces into his province. ONUC, under orders from Hammarskjöld, could not fight their way in. Both Lumumba and Kasavubu loudly denounced Hammarskjöld for not forcing Katanga to rejoin the Republic of the Congo. Finally Hammarskjöld, through negotiations, got ONUC troops into Katanga, but he still refused to use them to settle what he considered was an internal dispute, beyond the scope of the United Nations.

Patrice Lumumba flew into one of his ungovernable rages and asked Moscow for help. The Russians quickly supplied seventeen aircraft loaded with food and 400 men whom the Russians called "technicians," but whom the United States denounced as military advisers. President Kasavubu, who was strongly anti-Russian, denounced Lumumba's request to the Soviets and issued an order removing Lumumba as prime minister. Lumumba retaliated with an order removing Kasavubu as president.

The Congo government was now in a state of chaos, and Colonel Joseph Mobutu—the ex-army sergeant—seized power as military dictator. He achieved some measure of order, but ONUC had to post guards about the home of

Lumumba to prevent Mobutu from executing the former prime minister. Mobutu then expelled the Russians. This caused Valerian Zorin, Russian representative on the Security Council, to make a seventy-five minute speech to the Council, denouncing Dag Hammarskjöld. Zorin characterized the Secretary-General as a lackey for the Belgians and the West who were trying to reenslave the Congolese. He then vetoed a new Security Council resolution.

This was the tense situation when the General Assembly met in mid-September, 1960, for its fifteenth session. The diplomatic world was electrified when Nikita Khrushchev, Russian premier, suddenly announced that he would personally lead the Russian delegation to the fifteenth session of the United Nations. Immediately other world leaders announced that they also would attend the historic session. In all there were ten heads of state, eleven prime ministers, and twenty-eight foreign ministers. Among them, in addition to Khrushchev, were Nasser of Egypt, Sihanouk of Cambodia, Tito of Yugoslavia, Castro of Cuba, Macmillan of Great Britain, Sukarno of Indonesia, as well as Eisenhower of the United States.

The stage was set for a titanic battle.

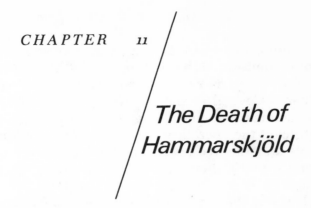

CHAPTER 11

The Death of
Hammarskjöld

The new session of the General Assembly began auspiciously with the admission and welcome of fourteen new nations, all of them, except Cyprus, from Africa. The others were Cameroon, Central African Republic, Chad, Congo (French Congo), Congo (Belgian Congo), Dahomey, Gabon, Ivory Coast, Madagascar, Niger, Somalia, Togo, and Upper Volta. Eight days later, on September 28, 1960, Mali and Senegal were added to the list of new members.

There was no objection to the admission of the former Belgian Congo, despite the disorder in the country and despite Lumumba's and Kasavubu's having sent opposing slates of delegates to the Assembly. The United States had balked at admitting Poland at the original meeting of the UN organization in 1946 because Poland lacked a stable government. But times had changed, and for political reasons it was considered desirable to admit the Congo despite its disorder and political instability.

Premier Khrushchev took the stage as the top star in the all-star session. The U.S. government had restricted his movements to the island of Manhattan for security reasons, although Khrushchev claimed the restriction was made because of American pique at the way he had broken off a planned Paris conference with President Eisenhower after an American U-2 spy plane was shot down over Russia. However, security did not prevent Khrushchev from holding press conferences from his balcony where each evening he exchanged banter and repartee with reporters who flocked around him.

His banter changed to viciousness on the floor of the General Assembly. In a ringing speech he denounced United Nations activity in the Congo and assailed Dag Hammarskjöld for exceeding his authority. The Secretary-General replied:

> Sometimes one gets the impression that the Congo operation is looked at as being in the hands of the Secretary-General, as somehow distinct from the United Nations. No; this is your operation, gentlemen. . . . There is nothing in the Charter which puts responsibility of this kind on the shoulders of the Secretary-General or makes him the independent master of such an operation. It was the Security Council which, without any dissenting vote, gave this mandate to the Secretary-General on 14 July.

Khrushchev attacked Hammarskjöld, accusing him of being unfit to hold the office of Secretary-General and proposing that the office be replaced with a three-man committee, which the Russian premier called a "troika" after the three-horse teams that pulled the old Russian sleds. In the Assembly hall the Secretary-General sits on a high dais to the right of the Assembly president. The speaker before the Assembly stands at a rostrum at a lower level and directly in front of the dais. So it was that

Hammarskjöld sat looking down at the back of the neck of the man who was trying to ruin him. He was impassive, as he always was in public. Only the way he fingered a pencil—a giveaway sign to his friends of his carefully concealed emotions—betrayed his feelings. It had been a Russian attack and boycott that had ruined Trygve Lie and forced the Norwegian's resignation as Secretary-General. The hushed delegates looked from the angry face of Khrushchev to the impassive face of the man he was attacking so viciously. Hammarskjöld had done more than any other single man to make the United Nations a force for peace. Many in Khrushchev's audience wondered if the destruction of Dag Hammarskjöld meant also the destruction of the United Nations.

In reply Hammarskjöld said:

> . . . the representative of the Soviet Union said that it is not proper for a man who has "flouted elementary justice to hold such an important post as that of Secretary-General." And later on he found reason to say to the delegates of this session that they should not "submit to the clamorous phrases pronounced here" by me "in attempts to justify the bloody crimes perpetrated against the Congolese people."
>
> I said the other day that I would not wish to continue to serve as Secretary-General one day longer than such continued service was, and was considered to be, in the best interest of the Organization. The statement this morning [of Premier Khrushchev] seems to indicate that the Soviet Union finds it impossible to work with the present Secretary-General.
>
> This may seem to provide a strong reason why I should resign. However, the Soviet Union has also made it clear that, if the present Secretary-General

were to resign now, they would not wish to elect a new incumbent but insist on an arrangement [the "troika"] which—and this is my firm conviction based on broad experience—would make it impossible to maintain an effective executive. By resigning, I would, therefore, at the present difficult and dangerous junction throw the Organization to the winds. I have no right to do so because I have a responsibility to all those States' Members for which the Organization is of decisive importance, a responsibility which overrides all other considerations.

It is not the Soviet Union, or, indeed, any other big power who needs the United Nations for their protection; it is all the others. . . . I shall remain at my post during the term of my office—

At this point the Secretary-General was interrupted by a standing ovation of the delegates. All members were on their feet except those of the Soviet bloc, who took their cue from a scowling Khrushchev who angrily drummed on his desk with his fists. A report said he banged with his shoe, but none of the photographs or television kinescopes of the event showed this.

Hammarskjöld lifted his hands for silence. His face was as impassive in this moment of victory as it had been when he was enduring Khrushchev's condemnation. He went on:

—as a servant of the Organization in the interests of all those other nations, as long as *they* wish me to do so.

In this context the representative of the Soviet Union spoke of courage. It is very easy to resign; it is not so easy to stay on. It is very easy to bow to the wish of a big power. It is another matter to resist. As is well known to all members of this Assembly, I have done so before on many occasions and in many directions. If it is the wish of those nations who see in the Organization their best protection in the present world, I shall now do so again.

The Assembly voted down Khrushchev's "troika" proposal. This was a victory for Hammarskjöld, but on the other side of the world, in the bloody Congo, he was suffering one major defeat after another. The economy of the African republic completely collapsed. Only urgent assistance from the UN kept thousands from starving. In October, 1960, the Secretary-General made a speech before the General Assembly in which he summed up what the United Nations was doing in this respect:

> In the vastness of the Congo, where so much movement depends on air services, everything would have been grounded in the last three months but for the air traffic control, the radio and navigation aids provided by the International Civil Aviation Organization, the International Telecommunication Union and the World Meteorological Organization [all UN affiliates]. Even the food and milk so generously provided by Member States for supply to children and refugees . . . have been largely carried in United Nations planes to country-wide distribution points where local authorities and Red Cross took over. . . .
>
> Hospitals abandoned by their medical staff have been quickly restored to use by medical units provided by Red Cross societies of many countries, and the elementary health services have been maintained by the World Health Organization. Plans for reopening schools . . . have largely depended on the

activities of the United Nations Educational, Scientific and Cultural Organization [UNESCO]. Plans for maintaining agricultural services are being developed. . . . All of these vitally essential services are rendered under the United Nations flag, thus eliminating any risk that they create a dependence of the Congo on any specific foreign power or that outside elements be permitted to establish what might develop into vested interests in the country.

Despite the vast humanitarian work being accomplished by the UN agencies in the Congo, the military and political situation was still in a state of chaos. Colonel Mobutu had achieved partial control of the mutinous army and was supporting President Kasavubu. In Katanga, Premier Moise Tshombe was still defying the central government. In this he was being aided by Belgium, and his rebel army was officered by mercenaries recruited from Belgium and other European countries. As a result a large number of Belgian business men and mine operators moved back into Katanga.

In the meantime, Lumumba escaped from his house arrest in Leopoldville and was recaptured by Mobutu. President Kasavubu assured Hammarskjöld that Lumumba would get a fair treason trial, but in January, 1961, Colonel Mobutu decided to turn Lumumba over to Tshombe in Katanga. ONUC officers asked Hammarskjöld for orders and were told that they were in no way authorized to interfere in Congo internal affairs. Lumumba, showing signs of severe beatings, was flown to Katanga. On February 13, 1961, Tshombe announced that Lumumba had been killed while trying to escape from his captivity.

Lumumba's murder brought a flood of censure on

Hammarskjöld, who continued to insist that he had no authority to interfere in the Congo's internal affairs. In the meantime, Kasavubu elevated his former minister of interior to the position of premier. This man, Cyrille Adoula, was a former labor leader and proved an efficient and selfless official. Mobutu agreed to confine his activities strictly to the army and to keep out of politics.

As the situation began to stabilize in the Congo, the secessionist state of Katanga was gripped by tribal jealousies and revolts against Tshombe. This was due to Tshombe's pro-Belgium policies and his support from pro-Belgium industrial interests who were trying to keep control of the richest part of the Republic of the Congo. It was clear that trouble in the Congo would not cease until the Europeans were removed and Tshombe's mercenary army disbanded. Tshombe bitterly resisted any attempt to extend United Nations peace-keeping activities in Katanga. In September, 1961, UN forces were attacked by tribal guerrillas. Twelve Italian aircrew men, helping operate transports for the UN, were slaughtered, and several other groups of UN noncombatants were captured. The result was greater condemnation of Hammarskjöld, who was doing all he could to bring order despite being hamstrung by conflict in the Security Council.

At the height of the fury Hammarskjöld personally went to the Congo where his attempts to see Tshombe were frustrated by the Katangan's refusal to talk to him.

In the Republic of Congo, Cyrille Adoula was proving an extremely able prime minister, while Tshombe was finding it increasingly difficult to put down the rebels in Katanga. Seeing control gradually slipping away, Tshombe agreed finally to talk with Hammarskjöld but refused to do so in Katanga. A meeting was arranged in Ndola, just across the Katangan border in Rhodesia. Hammarskjöld left Elizabethville, capital of the Republic of the Congo, on September 17, 1961, for a night flight to Ndola. As the UN plane approached the landing strip in Ndola, it inexplicably crashed, killing all aboard except one American sergeant who died later.

Immediately there were wild charges that the UN Secretary-General had been murdered. Several investigations were made, but nothing was ever proved. However, there is still considerable doubt that the crash was an accident.

The confrontation between East and West in the Congo held great danger of exploding into a world war. Both Russia and the United States realized this. Both proved their eagerness to keep the war from spreading by quickly agreeing on a successor to Dag Hammarskjöld. They agreed on a man known for his neutralist views. A Burmese, his name was Thant, and he was usually called U Thant. The Burmese have no surnames, and the U— which means "uncle" literally—is an honorific comparable to "honorable" in Western terms. Thant was born in 1909 in Pantanow, a town near Rangoon, Burma. Later he was headmaster of the National High School in his hometown. After World War II, U Nu became prime minister of Burma. U Thant had known U Nu when they were students at Rangoon University, and the new prime minister persuaded Thant to join the government. Thant became secretary for information and broadcasting after serving an apprenticeship in a lower position. He held this position until 1952 when he was sent to New York as a member of his country's delegation to the United Nations. This duty ended in 1953, but he returned in 1957 as his country's permanent delegate to the UN. He was still holding this position when he was elected acting Secretary-General on November 3, 1961, and permanent Secretary-General the following year.

After the death of Hammarskjöld the tragedy of the

Congo moved rapidly to a climax. Tshombe placed flowers on the dead Secretary-General's coffin and remarked, "It is sad," but the Katangan secessionist was still not ready to see his province reintegrated with the Congo. He agreed to a plan, based on Hammarskjöld's original idea, that U Thant presented. This would provide for a loose federation with Katanga as a self-governing province in the union of the Congo. However, Tshombe quickly showed that he had no real intention of accepting the plan.

The question now arises as to why the UN insisted on reintegrating secessionist Katanga with the Republic of the Congo. Adoula was bringing order into the republic. Why not let Katanga go her own way? The answer lies in the politics of the day. In the first place, the bulk of the Congo's wealth and tax base was in Katanga. Without the tax revenue from Katanga's mines, the Republic of the Congo could not sustain itself. In the second place, the United Nations had become an organization in which the membership was predominantly of small nations with the bulk of the members representing African and Asiatic nations. This was caused by the larger number of former colonies which had recently achieved independence. These African and Asiatic small nations were solidly opposed to Tshombe because of the support he and his mercenary army drew from Europeans with economic interests in Katanga's mines. They felt that an independent Katanga would be a Belgian colony in fact if not in name.

In the General Assembly each nation has a single vote regardless of size. Originally the UN had fifty-one members. By the time the Congo crisis reached its climax, there were twice as many members, and the big powers were no longer in control. With the Security Council deadlocked by East-West political maneuvering, the General Assembly was calling the turn. Even if the UN agreed to the split between Katanga and the Congo, fighting between the two could be expected to go on. At the same time it could well embroil adjoining African states, with the independent ones siding with the Congo and European-dominated ones like Rhodesia and the Union of South Africa supporting Tshombe. The result could well cause the fighting to spread throughout the continent.

Tshombe's control of Katanga was slowly slipping away as tribal revolts increased. In the meantime, U Thant suddenly faced a crisis far more serious than the Congo and its threat of an all-African war. The United States and Russia were in a confrontation that threatened a devastating nuclear war. It was a problem so serious that neither President John F. Kennedy of the United States nor Nikita Khrushchev of the Soviet Union could back down without a political loss of face that would have both domestic and world-wide repercussions. The United Nations was devised as a means of permitting the big nations to force peace on smaller nations. In a showdown between world nuclear powers, the United Nations was totally powerless, for it depended on the strength of the big powers to enforce UN decisions. When the United States and Russia approached the brink of war, there were no powers in the world strong enough to force these two nuclear giants to accept any UN directive.

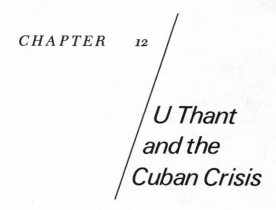

CHAPTER 12

U Thant
and the
Cuban Crisis

The Cuban crisis really began in January, 1959, when a revolutionary group led by Fidel Castro overthrew the dictator regime of Fulgencio Batista. Castro began his fight posing as an agrarian reformer, but once in power he revealed his Marxist policies. The United States was disturbed at having a Communist stronghold so close to U.S. shores and supported a counterrevolution launched by Cuban refugees in the United States. The counterrevolutionists' attempt to land at the Bay of Pigs in Cuba was a disastrous failure, exposing the United States to world condemnation.

While Castro was solidifying his position in Cuba, relations between the United States and Russia were worsening. Kennedy and Khrushchev met in Vienna in June, 1961, but were unable to come to an agreement on any subject. Relations between the two were badly strained over U.S. support of Mobutu, who had driven the Russian "technicians" from the Congo. The situation was further complicated by construction of the "Berlin Wall" to separate East and West Berlin. And the Russians were still greatly concerned about U.S. strategic aircraft and missiles located near the Russian border. Russia had earlier made a complaint in the UN about American nuclear-weapon-carrying planes flying close to the Russian border.

In the summer of 1962, Khrushchev began building secret intermediate-range ballistic rocket bases in Cuba. From this location nuclear warhead weapons could hit every major city in the United States. U.S. intelligence secured aerial photographs of this activity in October, 1962. Khrushchev denied that they were missile bases aimed at the United States, but President Kennedy ordered the U.S. navy to stop all arms shipments into Cuba. Such interference could be an act of war.

The United States, Russia, and Cuba all referred the crisis to the Security Council. Each knew that the Security Council was powerless, but the United Nations had long since become a propaganda forum from which a nation could put its side of a controversy before the world. The United States made it plain that she would accept no compromise that did not entail removal of the offending missiles from Cuba. A draft resolution submitted called for the UN Secretary-General to form a corps of observers to oversee the removal.

U Thant put off making any suggestions himself until he had time to consult with a large number of national delegates, and then he wrote letters to President Kennedy and Premier Khrushchev asking them to agree to voluntary suspension of the American quarantine of Cuba and the Russian missile shipments to give time for negotiations. Both Russia and the United States made a favorable response to U Thant, but on October 28 (five days after the crisis broke) Khrushchev suddenly agreed to remove the missiles already in place in Cuba. He also agreed to

UN supervision of the removals, but a furious Castro refused to permit UN observers into his country. U Thant made a trip to Cuba to see Castro but could not change the Cuban's mind. Castro was bitter toward Russia for withdrawing the missiles. The United States agreed to depend on aerial reconnaissance to verify the missile site deactivations, and by January, 1963, both the U.S. and Russia told the Security Council that the crisis had ended.

The extent of U Thant's involvement in settling the dispute has never been revealed. Outwardly, it appears to have been simply writing letters to Kennedy and Khrushchev and making a trip to Cuba to see Castro. However, one account claims that U Thant acted as a secret go-between in bringing Khrushchev and Kennedy to the final agreement to remove the Russian missiles from Cuba. In his annual report to the United Nations General Assembly, U Thant said that the United Nations—meaning himself—"aided" in averting a conflict between the Soviet Union and the United States.

The Cuban crisis did not relieve U Thant of his problems in the Congo. On Christmas Eve, 1962, Katangan troops suddenly attacked Elizabethville in an attempt to drive ONUC forces out of the Republic of the Congo. U Thant did not bother to inform the Security Council but, on his own authority, authorized the commander of ONUC forces in the Congo to take whatever measures he thought necessary to protect his troops. ONUC soldiers could protect themselves only by doing what they could not legally do—disarm the Katangan rebel army. This measure had been rejected by Hammarskjöld as illegal interference with the internal affairs of a UN member nation, which is specifically contrary to the UN Charter. U Thant, however, said his order did not cause ONUC to intervene in the Congo civil war but was simply an order to permit ONUC to protect itself when attacked.

As a result of U Thant's order, ONUC troops fought a hard battle with Katangan forces on December 29, and by January 5, 1963, were in control of Katanga province. This did not stop the fighting, since various tribes refused to cooperate with the central Congo government. To make matters worse, both France and Russia refused to pay their UN assessment to support the ONUC troops. Both claimed the General Assembly vote establishing ONUC was illegal because enforcement action was the prerogative of the Security Council only. The "Uniting for Peace" resolution only authorized the General Assembly to consider a question. The refusal to pay by France and Russia, plus the number of smaller nations who were in arrears on their peace-keeping assessments both for Suez and the Congo, brought the UN to the brink of bankruptcy. Total financial collapse was prevented by the sale of United Nations bonds and by assistance from the United States.

Finally, in 1964, the United States invoked Article 19 of the UN Charter which provides that any nation who is more than two years in arrears of UN payments should be denied a vote in the General Assembly and Security Council. The General Assembly refused to uphold the United States resolution for fear it would cause Russia and France to leave the UN. However, soon after this, Russia —while still refusing to pay the peace-keeping assessment —made a voluntary gift to the UN that was equal to the amount of the Russian assessment for the Congo operations.

The refusal or failure of so many nations to pay for UN peace-keeping forces caused more trouble when another UN Emergency Force was needed to prevent war in Cyprus. Soon after Cyprus gained independence, trouble broke out between the Christian Greek majority and the Moslem Turkish minority. Both Greece and Turkey took the side of their nationalities and war threatened. A resolution was adopted in the UN to send a peace-keeping force to Cyprus. All nations asked to supply troops refused because there were no UN funds to defray expenses. Finally the United States and Great Britain gave $3 million. Even then it was difficult to get neutral nations to furnish troops. A UN force was finally assembled but was ineffective, for it was forbidden to interfere with internal activities. The fighting did not stop until the Turks bombed the island, frightening the Cypriot Greeks into a cease-fire.

It had been Hammarskjöld's theory that a "UN presence" in an area of hostility would end fighting. This theory worked in Suez as long as the UN was present, but it failed in the Congo and Cyprus. In the two latter crises the fighting yielded only to force. It seems clear from this that UN peace-keeping forces cannot enforce peace unless they are prepared to fight as they did in Korea and—at the end—in the Congo. Such force, of course, is not practical when one or others of the big powers are directly involved as happened in Vietnam.

Vietnam began as a fight for independence from France. When the French were ousted in 1954, Vietnam was divided at the 17th parallel into a Communist-dominated North Vietnam and a republican (so-called) South Vietnam. Then, as happened earlier in Korea, the two Vietnams went to war with each other. The war did not begin as an invasion like the one that launched the Korean war but began as a guerrilla attack by the Viet Cong, a Communist-dominated revolutionary group that was aided by North Vietnam. When South Vietnam almost collapsed in 1963, President John F. Kennedy committed more U.S. aid and advisers as part of the United States policy to contain the expansion of Communism. Under President Lyndon B. Johnson this aid increased, and American troops were committed in larger and larger numbers.

The United Nations was unable to take action since its two strongest members—Russia and the United States—were arrayed against each other. However, U Thant—following the personal diplomacy pattern established by Hammarskjöld, did what he could through personal diplomacy. Since these were secret negotiations, very little has leaked out about them. It is known that Thant began trying to bring the United States and North Vietnam to the negotiating table as early as 1963. Leon Gordinker, professor of politics at Columbia University, in his book on the UN secretariat, said, "During 1965, [U Thant] secured an agreement from Ho Chi Minh [president of North Vietnam] to send an emissary to secret talks with a United States representative in Burma, but the United States government declined to make use of this possibility."

After this failure, Thant began to speak out in public on the Vietnam problem. At one time he said bitterly, "For various reasons, the role of the United Nations has been ignored or avoided in the settlement of some recent disputes, thus causing profound uneasiness in the minds of those who maintain that the United Nations represent the world's best hope of peace.

"A further drift in this direction, if not arrested in time, will mark the close of a chapter of great expectations and the heralding of a new chapter in which the world organization will provide merely a debating forum, and nothing else."

In this bitter speech, U Thant was not only denouncing the United States, Russia, and Israel—all of whom had ignored his best efforts at conciliation—but also Indonesia, who had tried to invade Malaysia, and Great Britain, who had announced the formation of the new republic of Malaysia before a fact-finding committee sent by U Thant could report on whether the people of North Borneo wanted to become a part of Malaysia.

The opening of 1967 brought renewed trouble in the uneasy truce in the Middle East. Syrian guerrillas kept attacking across the Israeli border, and the Israelis retaliated. The trouble came to a head on May 12 when Israel warned Syria that continued attacks by guerrilla forces would not be tolerated. A week later U Thant warned, "There has been a steady deterioration along the line between Israel and Syria, particularly with regard to disputes over cultivation rights in the Demilitarized Zone [between the two countries]."

At the same time Nasser of Egypt requested withdrawal of the United Nations Emergency Force which was patrolling along the Suez Canal, acting as a buffer between Israel and Egypt. The UNEF had been in place since the Suez crisis but had been stationed in Egypt because Israel had refused to permit the UN forces on its side of the border. Under these circumstances, the United Nations had no alternative but to remove the UNEF at Egypt's demand. Orders for the UNEF withdrawal were issued on May 18, 1967, although everyone knew that this would lead directly to a resumption of hostilities between Egypt and Israel. Nasser had had ten years since the end of the Suez fighting to rebuild his shattered army and air force and was now ready to resume the endless war.

The question has been asked many times since why U Thant ordered UNEF to withdraw without first calling an emergency session of the General Assembly to try to hold the peace-keeping force in place. There is no question but that the Secretary-General realized that withdrawal would lead to war again. In a cable to Nasser in Cairo, U Thant said:

> Irrespective of the reasons for the action you have taken, in all frankness, may I advise you that I have

serious misgivings for, as I have said every year in my annual reports to the General Assembly on UNEF, I believe this force has been an important factor in maintaining relative quiet in the area of its deployment during the past ten years and that its withdrawal may have grave implications for peace.

Since Israel had refused to accept the UN forces on its own soil in 1957 and none were forced on her, the United Nations had no legal right to force the presence of UN soldiers on Egypt. Egypt had accepted them in 1957 and had permitted them to remain for ten years. Now Egypt was demanding their removal. This U Thant felt obligated to do. Some observers believe that he should have convened the General Assembly and put all possible diplomatic pressure on Egypt to permit them to remain.

The situation became more heated when Nasser on May 22, 1967, refused to permit any more Israeli ships to pass through the Strait of Tiran into the Gulf of Aqaba. The Strait of Tiran and the Gulf of Aqaba separate the Sinai Peninsula and Saudi Arabia. This is the natural waterway to the Israeli port of Elath. Since Egypt had already closed the Suez Canal to Israeli ships, the blockade of the Strait of Tiran was an economic disaster to the Jewish nation and a challenge that the belligerent Israelis did not take lightly. They felt—and statements by the leaders of Syria, Jordan, and Egypt supported this belief —that the Arabs' intention was genocide—a complete extermination of Israel and its people.

The inevitable war finally broke on the morning of June 5, with fighting along the Gaza Strip—a tiny section of Arab land extending along the Mediterranean Sea into Israeli territory. Immediately Israeli land battalions struck at the 100,000-man army Egypt had deployed in the

Sinai Peninsula area. At the same time the Israeli air force destroyed most of the Egyptian air force on the ground before the enemy planes could get into the air.

The fighting sent a shock around the world. The Egyptian army had been armed by the Russians, and the United States was expected to support Israel. The situation was so tense that President Lyndon B. Johnson of the United States took advantage of the "hot line" to talk directly with Aleksei Kosygin, the Russian premier. The hot line is a telephone line strung at great expense across Europe to provide an emergency means for the leaders of the United States and Russia to confer when there is danger of immediate war.

Neither the United States nor Russia wanted war over the Middle East. They shifted the problem to the UN, where it was bogged down in endless debate. In the meantime, the determined Israelis ripped through the Arab defenses so rapidly that the war, for practical purposes, was won in three days. The fighting continued for three more days before an uneasy truce was effected.

The UN fighting now revolved around conditions for a permanent cease-fire. Israeli troops occupied the entire Sinai Peninsula and the divided city of Jerusalem and had driven Jordanian troops across the Jordan River. Arab and Russian peace demands included withdrawal of Israeli troops from this occupied Arab territory. But when it became painfully apparent that the Arab armies would completely collapse if the war continued, Nicolai Fedorenko, the Russian delegate to the Security Council, withdrew his country's demand that the Israelis relinquish their conquered territory before a cease-fire could be achieved.

The war was costly to the Arabs in terms of lives and territory, even though the fighting lasted only six days.

Israel occupied the formerly divided city of Jerusalem, the Jordanian land on the Israeli side of the Jordan River, and the Egyptian Sinai Peninsula. Thirty-five thousand Arabs were supposedly killed. Israeli losses were never made known. Saddest of all, this war settled nothing. Nasser died on September 28, 1971. His successor, President Sadat of Egypt, immediately renewed Nasser's threats against Israel. Diplomatic opinion was that Sadat realized the futility of another war with Israel but was being pushed by fanatic youth groups hysterically bent on avenging their country's national honor. Under these unstable conditions, it would be only a matter of time before blood again flowed in the Middle East, keeping alive a problem that the United Nations had ineffectively struggled to solve for more than a quarter century.

CHAPTER 13

The Agencies: Successes and Failures

While the General Assembly and the Security Council went on with their ineffectual bickering, other agencies of the United Nations went their own way—quietly working at their chartered tasks to help humanity. Some have been amazingly successful. Others have been as colossal a failure as the Security Council itself—and largely for the same reason: the refusal of the individual members of the UN to place national interest second to world welfare.

The outstanding failure has been the International Court of Justice. The Court is about twice as old as the United Nations, being a continuation of the Permanent Court of International Justice which was a part of the old League of Nations. Its legal operation is covered by a statute, based on the former court's statute, that is included as a part of the United Nations Charter. All members of the United Nations are members of the court, but membership in the court is also open to nonmembers of the UN who desire to join. Switzerland, Liechtenstein, and San Marino are three non-UN members who chose to join the court.

The court sits at The Hague in the Netherlands and is comprised of fifteen members elected by the General Assembly and the Security Council. Nine judges constitute a quorum, and questions are settled by a simple majority. The court's jurisdiction includes interpretations of treaties, questions involving international law, the existence of any fact which, if established, would constitute a breach of international obligation, and advisory opinions requested by the Security Council or the General Assembly. Other special UN agencies may ask for advisory opinions when authorized by the General Assembly. Decisions of the court are not compulsory unless the parties in dispute agree beforehand to accept the decisions of the court as compulsory.

The court's lack of means to enforce its decisions is the reason for its failure. The court heard its first case in 1946 when British warships were damaged by mines while passing through the Corfu Channel in Albanian waters. The area had previously been cleared by Allied mine sweepers. Great Britain charged that the Albanians had remined this stretch of international waters. The problem was referred to the Security Council, which suggested that Great Britain take the matter to the court. Albania objected but was overruled. While the Charter specifies that the disputants in a case must agree to the court's jurisdiction, Albania had made the mistake of already sending a letter to the court setting forth its position. The court ruled that this, in fact, acknowledged the court's jurisdiction in the case. In a decision handed down in 1949, the court ruled that Albania should pay reparations amounting to about $4 million. Albania refused to pay, and nothing could be done about it.

This initial case was followed by a number of relatively minor disputes, such as the question of whether Norway could restrict certain sea waters to her own fishermen, whether Colombia was right in granting political asylum to a Peruvian accused of staging a revolt in his home country, whether France could discriminate against American citizens in Morocco, and who owned two tiny islands in the channel between Great Britain and France. In 1951 Iran expropriated the Anglo-Iranian Oil Company owned by British interests. Private citizens and companies are not permitted to bring suit in the world court unless sponsored by their governments. Great Britain chose to support the Anglo-Iranian Oil Company on the grounds that the oil leases were based on international treaties. The court ruled that the expropriation of British oil wells by the Iranians did not come under the court's jurisdiction.

The court also refused to hear a United States complaint about treatment of U.S. aircrews forced to land in Hungary. Both Hungary and Russia rejected the court's jurisdiction in the case. In 1955, Great Britain tried to get the court to hear its complaint against Chile and Argentina over claims in Antarctica. Again, both countries involved angrily refused to accept the court's interference.

Even when countries agree to accept the court's jurisdiction, unfavorable decisions often cause bitterness that contribute to more international discord than the decision settled. A case in point was the argument in 1959, when Cambodia and Thailand quarreled over possession of the ruins of Temple Preah Vihear along their mutual border. The court ruled that the historical and religious site belonged to Cambodia. This infuriated the Thais, with resulting deterioration of relations between Cambodia and Thailand. If the decision had favored Thailand, Cambodia's reaction would have been the same, and the final results would have been identical. The loser will always be unhappy, and current nationalism will always make the court's efforts futile.

The court was not much more successful in its advisory opinions. In 1947, Russia insisted on "package deals" for admitting a new group of nations into the UN, and the General Assembly asked the court for an advisory opinion as to whether a member of the United Nations could make its consent to the admission of a new member dependent on conditions not expressly provided for in the Charter. (This question related to Russia's demand that Outer Mongolia be admitted to the UN before Russia would accept other nominees.)

The court ruled that conditions for admission to the UN were clearly outlined in the Charter. If these conditions were fulfilled, the Security Council should agree to admitting the applicant. Russia, however, refused to accept the advisory opinion and abstained from voting.

Russia also ignored another advisory opinion of the court. This involved the UN attempt to collect an assessment from members to support peace-keeping forces.

There are other organizations—some of them autonomous—which are "related" to the United Nations. The court is required by the UN Charter, but these related organizations were established under a portion of the UN Charter that authorizes agencies to be formed "by intergovernmental agreement and having wide international responsibilities, as defined in their basic instruments, in economic, cultural, educational, health and related fields."

Among these "intergovernmental agencies" are:

INTERNATIONAL ATOMIC ENERGY AGENCY

The IAEA was suggested by President Eisenhower in 1953, but was not formed until July, 1957. An autonomous group, IAEA's duties were listed in its statute as "seeking to accelerate and enlarge the contribution of atomic energy to peace, health, and prosperity throughout the world. It shall ensure, so far as it is able, that assistance . . . is not used in such a way as to further any military purposes."

Under this mandate IAEA has encouraged and given assistance to undeveloped countries who need nuclear power to make up for fuel deficiencies in generating electric power and for promoting the use of radioisotopes in medicine, agriculture, and industry. As natural fuels—coal, gas, and oil—are depleted, the use of nuclear generators will have increasing world importance.

INTERNATIONAL LABOR ORGANIZATION (ILO)

ILO was established in 1919 and became an autonomous organization associated with the League of Nations. In 1946 it became the first specialized agency associated with the United Nations. Its primary work is to raise international labor standards by building an International Labor Code. It also provides technical cooperation to governments with labor or social problems.

FOOD AND AGRICULTURE ORGANIZATION OF THE UNITED NATIONS (FAO)

FAO, whose permanent headquarters is in Rome, was organized in October, 1945, as an outgrowth of the UN Conference on Food and Agriculture which met in 1943. This is perhaps the most important of all the UN intergovernmental agencies, with the possible exception of the World Health Organization, for it strikes straight and hard at the problem of world starvation. The value to humanity of this agency's work alone justifies the existence of the UN and the money spent to maintain it.

FAO's operations cover a vast range. In North Africa FAO experts worked out a system to spray flying locust swarms with pesticide to save crops. In Burma they worked out storage systems that saved thousands of tons of rice from being lost each year. In Egypt's Nile delta they doubled rice production by introducing new seed and new methods of paddy farming. In India they increased farm production by seventy-five percent, again by introducing better methods. In Iran and other sections of the Middle East they worked out irrigation systems and found wells and water sources to open desert areas to cultivation. In Malaysia, Ceylon, and Peru they were able to double and triple the fish catches.

Nor is increased food growing FAO's only interest. It works with underdeveloped countries to build industries which help alleviate the food problem. One such project was help in constructing an Indian milk processing plant. Milk there comes primarily from buffaloes and is plentiful at certain periods and slack at others. The dehydration plant provides a way to keep the milk for use in the slack period. Animal disease control and reforestation (notably restoring the famed forests of the Cedars of Lebanon where Solomon got his timber) are other FAO projects.

UNITED NATIONS EDUCATIONAL, SCIENTIFIC, AND CULTURAL ORGANIZATION (UNESCO)

UNESCO, formed in 1946, is supposed to contribute to "peace and security by promoting collaboration among the nations through education, science, and culture, in order to further universal respect for justice, for the rule of law, and for the human rights and fundamental freedoms for all."

Although membership in the United Naitons carries with it the right to membership in UNESCO, nations not members of the UN may be admitted to membership as well. UNESCO's programs are not mandatory but are carried out in member states only at the request of governments and with their cooperation.

UNESCO's programs cover a wide range within its charter to provide educational, cultural, and scientific assistance. An example is a 1957 survey, *World Illiteracy at Mid-Century*, which UNESCO issued. The survey showed that about 700 million persons—forty-four percent of the world's population in 1950— were illiterate and that sixty-five percent were functionally illiterate. Functionally illiterate was defined as unable to read and write well enough to participate actively in a literate community. As a result of this study UNESCO established a far-reaching program to increase primary school enrollment and to improve curricula. This was particularly aimed at Latin American countries where the survey found that 17 million children lacked schools.

Another important UNESCO program is assistance in reclaiming arid land. In this program UNESCO makes available expert knowledge to assist developing nations and helps in establishing desert research stations in such countries as Algeria, West Africa, India, Israel, and the United Arab Republic where work is carried on to expand land for food production.

UNESCO, believing that the cultural gulf between peoples is an obstacle to understanding and good will, has initiated various programs of international discussions, social science studies, lecture tours by eminent intellectuals, and the translation of contemporary literary works in other languages.

UNESCO also fosters a series of programs in international exchange through fellowships and scholarships, and in mass communications.

WORLD HEALTH ORGANIZATION (WHO)

WHO ranks near FAO as the most important of the intergovernmental agencies associated with the UN. It acts as a coordinating authority for international health work, works to eradicate epidemics and diseases, promotes improved medical teaching standards, and fosters activities in the field of mental health. WHO must be given the major credit for a worldwide campaign to eradicate malaria, tuberculosis, venereal diseases in undeveloped countries, yaws in tropical areas, leprosy, and virus diseases. It has done extremely valuable work in environmental health, public health services, nursing, health education, cancer, nutrition, maternal and child health, and the control of narcotic drugs.

Other specialized agencies associated with the UN include the International Bank for Reconstruction and Development, International Development Association, International Finance Corporation, International Monetary Fund, International Civil Aviation Organization, Universal Postal Union, International Telecommunication Union, the World Meteorological Organization, and others. Each works toward international cooperation within its field.

Various economic commissions and assistance programs of the United Nations work in cooperation with or through these intergovernmental agencies.

Best known of all the United Nations agencies, outside the General Assembly and the Security Council, is the United Nations Children's Fund (UNICEF). It was originally created in 1946 as the United Nations International Children's Emergency Fund to aid children in the refugee camps following the end of World War II. When this work ended, UNICEF was continued as the United Nations Children's Fund to aid children in undeveloped and developing countries. By this time UNICEF was so well known that the acronym was retained although "International" and "Emergency" were dropped from the name. In a recent statement issued by UNICEF it was said:

> In the less developed countries of the world the number of children under 15 increased by about 257 million during the last 11 years, to the present total of some 1,052,000,000 (one billion, fifty-two million). In most developing countries, they comprise more than 40 percent of the population; in some, over half. And through the decade of the 1970s their numbers are expected to increase another 270 million.
>
> That is why UNICEF's concern has turned increasingly to the need to develop children, to give them an opportunity to realize their full growth, as it is an essential factor in the development of their countries.

UNICEF is aiding these children in many ways. In Asia, Africa, Latin America, and the Middle East, UNICEF has nutrition programs for preschool children. It is training teachers, because 450 million children in backward countries receive no schooling at all. It provides vaccine for tuberculosis, smallpox, typhoid fever, and penicillin to fight yaws and many infectious diseases.

There are thousands of stories about how UNICEF has aided individual children. This one is typical: "Two-and-a-half-year-old Parvathi lived in a village twenty miles from Hyderabad in India. When she was weaned, her mother put her on the regular family diet—rice and chilies with occasionally a little candy as a special treat," a UNICEF report said. "Parvathi hardly gained weight at all and she began to have trouble seeing when dusk set in.

"Finally, her mother took her to a UNICEF-aided nutrition clinic in the city of Hyderabad. The doctor took one look at the child's eyes and checked her into the hospital at once. She was suffering from an acute Vitamin A deficiency eye disease and would have gone blind in a few weeks. Massive doses of UNICEF Vitamin A saved Parvathi's sight."

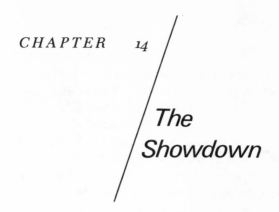

CHAPTER 14

The
Showdown

Maldives (officially Divehi) is the smallest independent nation in Asia, consisting of a number of coral islands off the southern tip of India. The reigning sultan rules over less than 100,000 people. After Maldives was granted independence from Great Britain in 1965, it applied for and was granted admission to the United Nations. The sultan, however, does not always take his country's UN membership seriously and sometimes sends a delegation and sometimes does not.

Although the total population of Maldives is about one-fifth that of the city of Indianapolis, Indiana, Maldives has one vote in the UN General Assembly. This gives its less than 100,000 people a voice as loud in terms of voting power as the 200 million-plus people of the United States or the estimated 600 to 800 million population of Red China or Russia's 244 million.

Maldives is not unique in the United Nations structure. In a speech made as part of the Dag Hammarskjöld Memorial Lectures, Dean Rusk, former U.S. secretary of state, said that a two-thirds majority of the UN General

Assembly represented only ten percent of the world's population. In such a situation, these so-called mini-states have it within their power to control the General Assembly. The importance of this is certainly not lost on the major powers. Since the passing of the "Uniting for Peace" resolution at the insistence of the United States, the General Assembly has gradually gained more and more power. Under the Charter, only the Security Council can authorize the use of force to back up UN demands. However, the Congo confusion is an example of how the General Assembly and the Secretary-General can direct matters when the Security Council is deadlocked. It will be remembered that in the Congo the General Assembly authorized the recruitment of a "peace-keeping" force— not a punitive or war-making army—to oversee truce activities. This peace-keeping force then became a fighting force at the end when ordered by the Secretary-General to "defend themselves." The effect was to put down the revolt in Katanga. This was in direct violation of the United Nations Charter, which specifies that the United Nations will not interfere in the internal affairs of a member. This is not to argue pro or con as to the moral justification for UN intervention but is strictly a statement based on the legalities of the Congo situation as interpreted from the UN Charter.

In the case of the Congo, the Afro-bloc in the United Nations was almost solidly arrayed against Katanga, for they considered Tshombe pro-European. Their support was the deciding factor in the General Assembly's backing of U Thant. There are now 132 members in the UN, and 78 of these can be classed as mini-states, with forty percent of the total membership made up of the Afro-Asian bloc alone. In his book *Is the United Nations Dead?* Benjamin Becker quotes a writer from the Chicago *Trib-*

une who said, "I wish the United Nations could work. I have come reluctantly to the view that in its present form it cannot. In the Assembly, the ultimate governing body of the United Nations, 5 percent of the world's population can carry the day against the other 95 percent, and 10 percent claim a two-thirds majority."

In discussing this problem Peter Benchley of *Newsweek Features* had this to say: "The result of this inequality is that when the United Nations tries to make a decision about almost anything, it is forced to behave like a giant tortured by gnats. As British writer Alistair Cooke noted a few years ago, the effect of the membership explosion has been 'to dissipate by sheer numbers the possibility of an effective consensus on anything.' "

No one expected this particular problem to arise. When the United Nations was formed, the Big Five expected to be big brothers to the smaller nations, keeping them in order while preserving peace by agreeing with one another. No one anticipated that the original 51-nation membership would grow to 132, with the expectation of adding another fifty or so in the next ten or fifteen years.

A number of these mini-states have little world responsibility and contribute nothing to the United Nations. As a result, there have been suggestions from time to time that small states with populations below a minimum figure (set everywhere from 100,000 to a million) would be permitted to have only an associate membership in the United Nations. This associate membership would not include a vote.

This plan, while discussed, has never been introduced as a resolution, for—as Peter Benchley points out—the big powers "have not dared press their point too hard because the very countries they would be offending by trying to demean their status are the same ones whose votes the big powers need to swing important decisions."

It was a fear of being outvoted by lesser nations that caused President Franklin D. Roosevelt and Premier Joseph Stalin to insist on the veto power for the five permanent members of the Security Council. This veto right will become increasingly important as the balance of power shifts in the General Assembly. Each of the Big Five, at one time or another, has utilized the veto to protect its national interest. This veto right is growing increasingly important, since it is the big nations' only protection in the UN against the hatred of the mini-nations.

In a speech delivered in 1963 Clement Attlee, former prime minister of Great Britain, said, "The root of trouble in today's world is that we believe . . . in the complete, or almost complete, right of every nation to do what it chooses. One still has the feeling that anything like a surrender of sovereignty is contrary to our human nature."

This belief in the welfare of one's own country over all others is nationalism. In assisting in the creation of so many new nations, the United Nations organization has encouraged the increase of nationalism in the world, with a resulting impact on the UN's own difficulty in bringing the world's nations together. Whether or not there is a danger in the proliferation of mini-states is a debatable question, but more and more observers seem to feel so. The great fear of nationalists is that the United Nations will start interfering in the internal affairs of its members —and even nonmembers. In this respect they point to the suppression of Katanga, which—in their view—had as much right to secede from the Congo as the American colonies had to declare independence from England. The Congo–Katanga affair was, according to this view, a purely internal affair to be settled between the two disputants.

Balancing this belief is the claim that the Congo mess was in danger of embroiling the world in a global war and, therefore, it was the UN's duty to involve itself in the dispute. This argument overlooks the point that no internal war in any country can involve major nations unless those big powers *want* to be involved because they feel that their own national interests are tied to one of the sides. So again we come back to nationalism as the source of the trouble.

Another example given by extreme nationalists as interference by the UN in internal affairs of a member is the long-standing dispute over apartheid (total separation of races) in Rhodesia and South Africa. Rhodesia was originally a British colony brought into the Commonwealth by the empire builder Cecil Rhodes in 1888. The colony broke away from Great Britain in 1965 in a dispute over the rights of natives. In doing so Rhodesia became the first British colony to leave the Commonwealth without consent since the independence of the American colonies in 1776. Rhodesia's white population, which comprises only five percent of the total population, controls the country, and the break with Great Britain was caused by British attempts to give the ninety-five-percent-black majority an increased voice in their country's government.

Great Britain, claiming the secession illegal, imposed trade restrictions on Rhodesia. The Security Council— although there was no threat to international peace— likewise passed a resolution asking UN member nations to impose trade sanctions and refuse to trade with Rhodesia. The embargo against Rhodesia was a failure. Although the Afro-Asian majority bloc in the UN demanded that the United Nations use force to oust the white supremacy government, none of the big powers were prepared to go to this extreme. The Rhodesia boycott, voted by the predominantly Afro-Asian bloc, failed because most UN members refused to stop trading with Rhodesia—*even though many of them voted for the boycott resolution.*

Rhodesia is rich in gold, chrome, asbestos, coal, copper, tin, and precious stones. These and agricultural products continue to circulate in the world market despite the UN boycott. In 1972 the United States representative in the UN complained that a number of nations—whom he charitably neglected to name—were violating the boycott. The violations will continue, because Rhodesian trade is profitable and in some cases essential to her neighbors in Africa.

The South African problem is a different matter. South Africa, the nation occupying the southern tip of Africa, has been embroiled in racial troubles since the beginning of the UN. Several times India has complained to the UN about the treatment of South Africans of Indian descent, and the Afro-Asian bloc has been unceasing in its demands for reprisals against South Africa's apartheid policy. This policy perpetuates total separation of races, restriction of the minority to menial jobs, lack of educational opportunities, and complete violation of civil rights.

Despite the apartheid policy in South Africa, the UN did not see fit to apply economic sanctions against South Africa as it did against Rhodesia. The attack on South Africa came from a different angle. Here the long-running battle has been over South Africa's control of the province of South West Africa. South West Africa was taken from Germany at the end of World War I and given to South Africa under a League of Nations mandate. When the League of Nations was dissolved after World War II, South Africa applied for permission to annex the province. This was refused and a demand made for South Africa to place the province under a UN trusteeship. Under such a trusteeship, South Africa would govern South West Africa only until the province was sufficiently developed to govern itself. During the trusteeship period, South Africa would be required to submit reports and permit inspections to ensure that the trustee territory was being prepared for independence.

South Africa refused, claiming that the United Nations had no jurisdiction over South West Africa. In 1950, the United Nations referred the dispute to the International Court of Justice. The court found that the UN had no authority to dissolve the old League of Nations mandate and that South West Africa was not ready for self-government. It did rule that South Africa was required to submit reports to the UN and to prepare South West Africa for independence. South Africa refused to submit such reports or to permit UN inspections. Ethiopia and Liberia then asked the court to rule that South Africa's apartheid policy violated its mandate and that the mandate be dissolved for this reason. (The problem was shunted to the court because the treatment of a minority or a majority by a minority government is an internal affair. The UN Charter specifically prohibits the UN from interfering in internal affairs of a nation.)

The Ethiopia-Liberia request was filed in 1960. No decision was forthcoming until 1966, when the court rejected the case as a South African internal matter, outside the court's jurisdiction. There is no legal justification for any interference by the court or the UN in the internal operations of a member state, the Court ruled, unless such action endangers world peace. The angry Afro-Asian bloc in both 1966 and 1967 pushed resolutions through the General Assembly to end South Africa's control over South West Africa and to set up an independence commission to run the province until it was ready for self-government. South Africa defied the resolutions, but nothing could be done about the situation. The big powers on the Security Council did not want to use force and involve themselves in another mess like the Congo crisis.

It can be seen from this that the growing power of the mini-states, which some observers profess to fear, is not decisive. While they may have the votes to push through their desires in the form of resolutions, they do not have the military and financial power to back them up. They must depend on the big powers for these essentials. If the big powers see no national advantage to themselves in taking drastic action, nothing will be done.

This is not to say that the mini-nations do not wield tremendous power with their vote advantage. This the United States found out when the showdown came over the seating of Red China in the United Nations. When the UN was formed in 1945, China was controlled by Chiang Kai-shek's Kuomintang government. In 1948 Mao Tse-tung's Communist government gained control of the entire Chinese mainland, forcing Chiang into exile in Taiwan. Chiang insisted, and has maintained the fiction ever since, that his government was the only legal Chinese government. It will be remembered that soon after the evacuation of Chiang Kai-shek from the Chinese mainland, the Russian delegate demanded that the Nationalist Chinese be expelled from the UN and China's seat given to the Red Chinese. This was voted down under United States leadership, and the U.S. continued to block Red Chinese entry into the United Nations until 1971.

The problem was not one of merely admitting Red China to membership. Red China was not asking for *membership*. China had UN membership and was a charter member of the United Nations. Both Mao Tse-tung in Red China and Chiang Kai-shek in Taiwan agreed that there was only one China. At no time was there a question of there being two Chinas. The argument was over which of the Chinese governments—the government in exile on Taiwan or the Red Chinese government which ruled the mainland with its 800 million [estimated] people—represented the Chinese people as a whole. Chiang's argument was that the Mao Tse-tung government was illegal and would soon be overthrown when the Nationalist Chinese invaded the mainland. The Russian argument was that there had been a revolution in China and that the Mao government—having won the battle—was now the legal government of China.

By the end of 1970, it was apparent to the United States that world sentiment was in favor of admitting Red China to the United Nations. As a result, U.S. strategy shifted to a policy of no longer trying to keep Red China out of the UN. In the words of McGeorge Bundy, who represented the U.S. at the UN, "the heart of the matter was not seating Red China, but to prevent the expulsion of Nationalist China."

The debate on the question came to a head in October, 1971. The United States, faced with defeat, moved that a question of such importance as expelling a delegation should be considered only by a three-quarter majority rather than a simple majority. This was rejected by an overwhelming vote in the General Assembly, overshadowing the expulsion of the Nationalist Chinese on the next vote. The expulsion resolution was sponsored by Albania, Algeria, Ceylon, Congo, Cuba, Equatorial Guinea, Guinea, Mali, Mauritania, Nepal, Pakistan, Rumania, Somalia, Southern Yemen, Syria, Sudan, Tanzania, Yugoslavia, and Zambi.

The resolution read:

> The General Assembly,
> Recalling the principles of the Charter of the United Nations—
> Considering that the restoration of the lawful

rights of the People's Republic of China is essential both for the protection of the Charter of the United Nations and for the cause that the United Nations must serve under the Charter

Recognizing that the representatives of the Government of the People's Republic of China are the only lawful representatives of China to the United Nations and that the People's Republic of China is one of the five permanent members of the Security Council

Deciding to restore all the rights of the People's Republic of China and to recognize its Government as the only legitimate representative to the United Nations and to expel representatives of Chiang Kaishek from the place they unlawfully occupy at the United Nations and in all the organizations affiliated with it.

The vote was seventy-six to thirty-five with seventeen abstainers. The *New York Times* reported that "pandemonium broke out on the Assembly floor. The representative of Tanzania, in the front row, danced a victory dance in front of the rostrum." In other parts of the hall there were shouts of glee and cheers from delegates of various mini-states. Remarks were heard that the United States had at last been put in her place.

President Richard Nixon was quoted as being deeply angered and concerned about the obvious hatred of the United States shown by so many of the mini-states. The disturbing thing was that this hatred came not only from the Communist bloc nations but also from many who had been or were still receiving considerable economic aid from the United States. This unprecedented display of anti-American sentiment caused bitter repercussions in

Congress. Indignant senators and representatives slashed some of the proposed foreign aid bill funds and threatened to cut more. Some even went so far as to advocate that the United States leave the UN. There was considerable resentment, also, because many felt that the United States' friends had "betrayed" her in voting for the resolution to unseat Chiang Kai-shek's delegation.

The UN We Believe organization, a group of businessmen devoted to getting American industry support for the UN, canvassed several UN ambassadors from countries friendly to the United States to see why they voted against this country.

The Canadian representative replied:

> The basis of the Canadian position on the China question was that states and not governments are members of the United Nations. Clearly, there cannot be two governments of the same state. China as a state was already a member, and the only issue with which the United Nations had to deal was who should represent China. This has nothing to do with size, ideology of the government in power. Clearly, the government in Peking is the Government of China, and the claim of the Government of Taipei to be the Government of China is untenable. It would be beyond the powers of the General Assembly to decide that China was divided, and that two governments should therefore divide the existing China seat, especially since neither Peking nor Taipei claimed that the representation of more than one state was involved. As it was in its power to do, the General Assembly decided that the representation of the People's Republic of China was legally entitled to occupy the single China seat.

The Dutch ambassador replied:

It is the view of the Netherlands government that for the lessening of political tensions in the world it is desirable and even indispensable that the People's Republic of China participate in the deliberations of the United Nations, by occupying the seat available to the government of China.

Great Britain's position was this:

The General Assembly did not act to "expel" a member state. The state of China had been a member of the UN from the beginning. Neither the Government of the People's Republic of China nor the authorities on Taiwan had accepted the concept that both should be represented, and the United Nations was obliged to choose between two rival claimants. Britain chose the government of nearly a quarter of the human race, believing its participation in the international community to be both right and necessary.

These reasons are well considered and logical. Then why did the United States fight so hard for so many years to keep Red China out of the United Nations? While Red China has been a disruptive force in world politics, the purpose of the United Nations is to provide a "world forum" where disputes can be fought with words instead of bullets. It would seem that the inclusion of the Red Chinese in the UN would, as both Britain and the Netherlands pointed out, be an important step toward peace in the world today.

No doubt the government of the United States understood this situation very well. Unfortunately, the U.S. had supported Chiang Kai-shek since before World War II and could not readily abandon him without leaving the impression with other international friends that U.S. friendship was not reliable. Also, the United States and Red

China were on opposite sides in the long-drawn-out struggle in Vietnam. American suspicion of communism played a part as well. In addition, Chiang Kai-shek had considerable support from a number of influential members of Congress. Chiang, who professed the Protestant religion, was strongly supported by some American religious groups who saw in his assertion that he would return to mainland China a means of combatting the godlessness in China.

The fight over the seating of Red China was followed by the refusal of U Thant to consider a third term as Secretary-General. The Burmese diplomat had served for ten years and was suffering from severe ulcers. He resigned effective December 31, 1971, and was replaced by Kurt Waldheim of Austria, who was elected without the usual fight that centered around selection of a Secretary-General. Waldheim, an experienced and smooth diplomat, was quite a different man from the three Secretary-Generals who had preceded him. He was born in 1918, the son of an Austrian schoolteacher, and grew up to become a lawyer. He was sufficiently high in political circles to be appointed his country's permanent representative when Austria was admitted to the UN in 1955. He then returned to Austria to take over as foreign minister under the Conservative party leadership. After two years in this office, Waldheim came back to the United Nations as Austria's permanent representative, holding this post until he was chosen to succeed U Thant. He has the reputation for being extremely diplomatic and having a special talent for conciliation. He is expected to be quieter than his three predecessors and not as likely to be so eager to increase the prestige of the Secretary-General's office. His term of office extends to December 31, 1976.

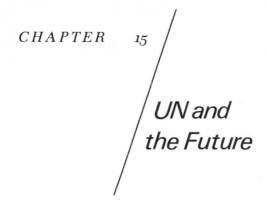

CHAPTER 15

UN and the Future

The United Nations has had sufficient success to justify its existence, but even its most enthusiastic supporters must admit that the organization has fallen far short of achieving the ideals set forth in its Charter. However, the fact that the United Nations has survived for more than a quarter of a century is proof of a sort that its quarreling members want it to continue. This is true even of Russia, who has been accused of being the most obstructive of all the member nations. Whenever Russian delegations walked out of the UN, they always returned. In the crisis over the UN budget, Russia, rather than see the UN collapse for lack of money, made a "voluntary gift" equal to the assessment she refused to pay. It appears as if all the important members agree in principle with an observation that appeared in the *New Yorker* magazine some years ago: "The United Nations, which in its present form is a league of disunited nations . . . is our last chance to substitute order for disorder, government for anarchy . . . we had better make it good."

Just what turn the United Nations will take in the immediate years to come is difficult to predict. Some things seem evident. The smaller nations will continue to press for a revision of the veto article in the Charter. In this respect Adam Malik of Indonesia, the UN General Assembly president in 1971, gave an interview in Singapore in January, 1972, in which he said:

> Every organization has its flaws, and the UN is no exception. One I would like to see remedied is the veto system. I have had the experience of working with the Assembly's members throughout the day and far into the night in order to hammer out a resolution—only to have it vetoed in the Security Council, a body consisting of only five nations. Five very big nations to be sure.
>
> So a decision that can be nearly unanimous in the General Assembly after many hours of deliberation and hard work can be upset by a veto from just one nation.
>
> If there is any one flaw in the United Nations, it is this. And I can tell you now that there is widespread feeling in the General Assembly that the United Nations Charter will have to be changed. But, of course, we all realize that the superpowers will probably be opposed to any change that would dispossess them of the veto—even China.

Adam Malik's condemnation of the veto came just three weeks after vetoes in the Security Council prevented the UN from taking any positive action in a sudden outbreak of war between India and Pakistan. Pakistan was formed from India at the end of World War II, being created to separate predominantly Moslem areas from predominantly Hindu India. This separation created Pakistan in two parts—East and West Pakistan—which were separated by the bulk of India. In 1970 the two Pakistans became embroiled in civil war when East Pakistan seceded, calling itself Bangladesh. India invaded Bangladesh when it appeared that Pakistan was going to put down the revolt. Russia immediately supported India's invasion to aid the rebel Bangladesh government. The United States and China sided with Pakistan. As a result, Russia three times vetoed Security Council cease-fire resolutions. This deadlocked the Security Council, and the problem was shifted to the General Assembly under the "Uniting for Peace" resolution.

The General Assembly immediately voted a cease-fire and called for India to withdraw her troops from Bangladesh on December 7, 1970. India ignored the resolution, continuing to fight until the Pakistani army in Bangladesh surrendered on December 16. This insured Bangladesh's independence from Pakistan. Later, in 1972, Bangladesh applied for membership in the United Nations. The Chinese representative to the UN then cast Red China's first veto to prevent Bangladesh's admission. Still later in the year China cast another veto when the question of Bangladesh's admission was again raised.

Equally futile was an attempt by world airline pilots to get the United Nations Security Council to take action against nations harboring skyjackers of transport aircraft.

President Richard Nixon suggested, in a foreign policy speech, that the UN Secretary-General take over more of the day-to-day peace-keeping activities from the Security Council. Waldheim declined, telling newsmen that it was up to the Security Council to meet peace-keeping problems.

"I can't exert force on member nations," he said. "But I believe the Secretary-General has the moral authority to exercise his influence." Unlike Hammarskjöld and U

Thant, Waldheim refused (at the same interview) to give his views on the Vietnam War, further indicating that he intended to avoid controversy that might cause his boycott by a major power as Trygve Lie and Dag Hammarskjöld had been boycotted by Russia.

Future United Nations operations in fields outside peace keeping are sure to be handicapped by the UN's growing deficit. In 1972 the UN Environment Conference, held in Stockholm, made some progress but became bogged down in international politics and national fears. The Chinese delegation demanded that both the United States and Russia be branded "world polluters" because of their nuclear policies. A group of Black African nations (calling themselves the Dakar bloc) held up agreement on a resolution with a demand that it include provisions for reparations to them for the "rape of Africa." And most serious of all was the disagreement of various nations on future UN pollution control.

Small developing nations were the major opponents of any binding agreements on world pollution. They felt that it was difficult enough for them to attract industry and capital needed for their development without adding a high financial burden of pollution control on interested companies. The manager of a steel mill in Sweden told the UN Pollution Conference that he was being undersold by a company in Norway because Sweden has high pollution control requirements and Norway has none.

Here again we see national needs and policies conflicting with world welfare. In considering the roadblocks nationalism has placed in the way of UN basic policies, it has been suggested that the United Nations today is much like the United States was when the latter was formed in 1776. Then the individual states were independent units that banded together for mutual support, while continuing to maintain their individual state governments. From this beginning there was a violent argument as to whether the union should be a loose federation, with the federal authority exercising little power, or a strict federation, with the federal government supreme and the states subservient to it. It required a bloody civil war to establish federal authority in the United States. We have a somewhat similar situation in the UN today. The sovereign states who joined the UN have retained their national authority. It is not likely that they will relinquish this authority to the UN without a world war similar to the U.S. civil war.

The fear of a United Nations dictatorship was very much in the minds of the founders of the United Nations. It was also a fear expressed in the United States while the U.S. Senate was debating the ratification of the UN Charter. Creation of such a UN dictatorship is not possible so long as the veto principle remains. Any one of the five permanent members of the Security Council could—and surely would—block any action that would be contrary to its desires.

A dictatorship is maintained in every case by force. A coalition of smaller nations in the UN, regardless of their preponderance in the voting, has no power to enforce its demands. Enforcement can legally be done only by the Security Council. The General Assembly does not have an army. In the Congo the General Assembly *invited* member nations to supply peace-keeping forces. In Korea the Security Council did the same thing. In neither case was any country ordered to supply troops.

The question has arisen as to the desirability of raising a United Nations military force as a standing army to be ready for either peace-keeping activities or for enforcement. A standing UN army could be under the orders of the Security Council's military staff committee or the Secretary-General. It will be remembered that when the possibility of a UN army was discussed in the early months of the Korean War, General Douglas MacArthur indicated to Trygve Lie that he would be available to command such an army. However, a UN army, if strong enough militarily to challenge any one of the superpowers, could conceivably lead to a dictatorship under the right conditions. The establishment of such an army is therefore a very remote possibility.

Another thing that hampers the United Nations is its insolvency. Even though Secretary-General Waldheim has committed himself to "austere budgets" in the future, there still are insufficient funds to maintain the UN's budget. The last released figures on UN contributions showed that the ten top contributors were:

United States	$ 276,332,665
Great Britain	48,544,890
Russia (not the Soviet states of Byelorussia and the Ukrainian S.S.R., which hold individual memberships of their own)	41,998,270
Sweden	35,602,924
Canada	34,338,811
France	27,471,830
Denmark	22,296,184
Italy	20,075,798
Japan	18,688,221
Netherlands	15,670,052

Of the total 132 members, only 41 give more than a million dollars in dues. Contributions from the other countries range from Cuba's $871,288 to Equatorial Guinea's $5,011.

It can be seen from this that the United States is the financial backbone of the UN and that a United States pullout from the world organization, as some advocated after the U.S. defeat on the expulsion of Nationalist China, would financially wreck the United Nations. Such a pullout is not likely, nor is it likely that Russia or any of the other major powers will desert the UN. Once there was a question as to whether any country could quit the UN or whether the majority would force the secessionist to remain as the American Civil War was fought to prevent the Southern states from withdrawing from the Union. However, when Indonesia resigned from the UN, not a single voice was raised in protest. Indonesia resigned for the sole purpose of making it easier for Indonesian President Sukarno to attack Malaysia. When Indonesian aggression failed and Sukarno was deposed, Indonesia applied for reinstatement and was accepted back into the UN.

While admittedly the UN has not been effective, it has made major accomplishments. It has been slow to act and often proved powerless. However, it must be given credit for its humanitarian work and for stopping some small wars that might well have grown into world confrontations with disastrous results. These efforts alone more than justify the existence of the United Nations. Even without these accomplishments, the UN would still be worthwhile as an organization where angry nations can talk and concerned people can try to bring them together.

The important thing about the United Nations is not what it has been, or what it is, but what it can become. As it was pointed out in the Rockefeller Panel Report on U.S. Foreign Policy (1959), "The United Nations stands, finally, as a symbol of world order that will be built. To measure the UN's contributions, one needs to ask how much meaner and poorer, how much less touched by home or reason, would be the world scene if it suddenly ceased to exist."

Important Dates in United Nations History

Atlantic Charter forecasts United Nations	August 14, 1941
Declaration by the United Nations is first public use of name "United Nations"	January 1, 1942
Dumbarton Oaks Conference lays groundwork for the United Nations Charter	August–October, 1944
Yalta Conference reconciles Russian and U.S. views on future United Nations	February 11, 1945
San Francisco Conference adopts UN Charter	June 26, 1945
First session of General Assembly held in London	January, 1946
Iran lodges first complaint to Security Council	January 19, 1946
Partition of Palestine	November 29, 1947
Czechoslovakia government overthrown by Communists. UN action blocked by Russia	February 22, 1948
State of Israel proclaimed; Arabs attack	May 14, 1948
Count Folke Bernadotte, UN mediator in Palestine assassinated in Jerusalem	September 17, 1948
Berlin blockade, which began in August, brought to Security Council attention	September 29, 1948
Universal Declaration of Human Rights voted	December 10, 1948

/ 175

U.S.S.R. demands Nationalist China relinquish seat in UN to Communist China, precipitating boycott of Security Council by Russia which made Korean War possible	January 8, 1950
South Korea invaded, beginning Korean War	June 25, 1950
Security Council Resolution involves UN in Korean War	June 27, 1950
Dag Hammarskjöld elected Secretary-General to replace Trygve Lie, who resigned	April 10, 1953
Korean War armistice signed	July 27, 1953
First UN International Conference on Peaceful uses of atomic energy	August 8, 1955
Independence for numerous African states	1956 through 1960
Egypt nationalizes Suez Canal, precipitating a renewal of Middle East crisis	July 26, 1956
Anti-Communist uprising in Hungary; UN powerless to act	October 22, 1956
Israel invades Egypt	October 29, 1956
UN cease-fire order in Middle East crisis vetoed in Security Council by France and England	October 30, 1956
United Nations Emergency Force plan adopted to over-	

see Middle East truce | November 4, 1956

Independence of Congo triggers trouble | June 30, 1960

Secession of Katanga launches Congo civil war | July 12, 1960

UN Emergency Force organized to enforce peace in the Congo | July 13, 1960

Fifteenth session of the General Assembly opens with the greatest collection of heads of states ever assembled in history | September 20, 1960

Khrushchev promotes "troika" plan to replace Secretary-General in UN | September 23, 1960

Dag Hammarskjöld killed in plane crash while in the Congo | September 13, 1961

Russian missiles in Cuba cause new crisis | October, 1961

U Thant of Burma elected to succeed the late Dag Hammarskjöld | November 3, 1961

Katanga troops attack ONUC forces, resulting in order for UN forces to fight back | December 25, 1962

UNEF peace-keeping force leaves Egypt, opening way for renewed war in Middle East | May 18, 1967

Israelis denied access to Gulf of Aqaba | May 22, 1967

Six Day War begins between

Israel and Egypt	June 5, 1967
UN General Assembly votes to seat Red China and to expel Nationalist China	October 23, 1971
U Thant declines a third term as Secretary-General; Kurt Waldheim elected to succeed him	December 31, 1971

APPENDIX B

UN Memberships

Current membership (1973) of the United Nations is 132 members. The date of admission is listed after each member, with the exception of the charter members (51 nations) who participated in the founding of the world organization.

Afghanistan (1946)
Albania (1955)
Algeria (1962)
Argentina
Australia
Austria (1955)
Bahrain (1971)
Barbados (1966)
Belgium
Bhutan (1971)
Bolivia
Botswana (1966)
Brazil
Bulgaria (1955)
Burma (1948)
Burundi (1962)

Byelorussian S.S.R.
Cambodia (1955)
Cameroon (1966)
Canada
Central African Republic (1960)
Ceylon (1955)
Chad (1960)
Chile
China
Colombia
Congo (Brazzaville) (1960)
Costa Rica
Cuba
Cyprus (1960)
Czechoslovakia

Dahomey (1960)
Denmark
Dominican Republic
Ecuador
Egypt (United Arab Republic)
El Salvador
Equatorial Guinea (1968)
Ethiopia
Fiji (1970)
Finland (1955)
France
Gabon (1960)
Gambia (1965)
Ghana (1957)
Great Britain
Greece
Guatemala
Guinea (1958)
Guyana (1966)
Haiti
Honduras
Hungary (1955)
Iceland (1946)
India
Indonesia (1950)
Iran
Iraq
Ireland (1955)
Israel (1949)
Italy (1955)
Ivory Coast (1960)
Jamaica (1962)
Japan (1956)

Jordan (1955)
Kenya (1963)
Kuwait (1963)
Laos (1955)
Lebanon (1966)
Lesotho (1966)
Liberia
Libya (1955)
Luxembourg
Malagasy Republic (1960)
Malawi (1964)
Malaysia (1957)
Maldives (1965)
Mali (1960)
Malta (1964)
Mauritania (1961)
Mauritius (1968)
Mexico
Mongolia (1961)
Morocco (1956)
Nepal (1955)
Netherlands
New Zealand
Nicaragua
Niger (1960)
Nigeria (1960)
Norway
Oman (1971)
Pakistan (1947)
Panama
Paraguay
Peru
Philippine Commonwealth

Poland
Portugal (1955)
Qatar (1971)
Rumania (1955)
Russia (U.S.S.R.)
Rwanda (1962)
Saudi Arabia
Senegal (1960)
Sierra Leone (1961)
Singapore (1965)
Somalia (1960)
South Africa
Southern Yemen (1967)
Spain (1955)
Sudan (1956)
Swaziland (1968)
Sweden (1946)
Syria
Tanzania (1961)

Thailand (1946)
Togo (1960)
Trinidad and Tobago (1962)
Tunisia (1956)
Turkey
Uganda (1962)
Ukrainian S.S.R.
United Arab Emirates (1971)
United States
Upper Volta (1960)
Uruguay
Venezuela
Yemen (1947)
Yugoslavia
Zaire Republic (formerly Congo—Kinshasa) (1960)
Zambia (1964)

APPENDIX C

The Universal Declaration of Human Rights

Note: This is the English translation as published by the U.S. State Department in January, 1949.

Preamble

Whereas, recognition of the inherent dignity and of the equal and inalienable rights of all members of the human family is the foundation of freedom, justice and peace in the world,

Whereas disregard and contempt for human rights have resulted in barbarous acts which have outraged the conscience of mankind, and the advent of a world in which human beings shall enjoy freedom of speech and belief and freedom from fear and want have been proclaimed as the highest aspiration of the common people,

Whereas it is essential, if man is not to be compelled to have recourse, as a last resort, to rebellion against tyranny and oppression, that human rights should be protected by rule of law,

Whereas it is essential to promote the development of friendly relations between nations,

Whereas the peoples of the United Nations have in the Charter reaffirmed their faith in fundamental human rights, in the dignity and worth of the human person and in the equal rights of men and women and have determined to promote social progress and better standards of life in larger freedom,

Whereas, Member States have pledged themselves to achieve, in cooperation with the United Nations, the promotion of universal respect for and observance of human rights and fundamental freedoms,

Whereas a common understanding of these rights and freedoms is of the greatest importance for the full realization of this pledge,

Now therefore,

The General Assembly,

Proclaims this Universal Declaration of Human Rights as a common standard of achievement for all peoples and all nations, to the end that every individual and every organ of society, keeping this Declaration constantly in mind, shall strive by teaching and education to promote respect for these rights and freedoms and by progressive measures, national and international, to secure their universal and effective recognition and observance, both among the peoples of Member States themselves and among the peoples of territories under their jurisdiction.

ARTICLE 1

All human beings are born free and equal in dignity and rights. They are endowed with reason and conscience and should act towards one another in a spirit of brotherhood.

ARTICLE 2

Everyone is entitled to all the rights and freedoms set forth in this Declaration, without distinction of any kinds, such as race, color, sex, language, religion, political or other opinion, national or social origin, property, birth or other status.

Furthermore, no distinction shall be made on the basis of the political, jurisdictional or international status of the country or territory to which a person belongs, whether it be independent, trust, non-self-governing or under any other limitation of sovereignty.

ARTICLE 3

Everyone has the right to life, liberty and the security of person.

ARTICLE 4

No one shall be held in slavery or servitude; slavery and the slave trade shall be prohibited in all their forms.

ARTICLE 5

No one shall be subjected to torture or to cruel, inhuman or degrading treatment or punishment.

ARTICLE 6

Everyone has the right to recognition everywhere as a person before the law.

ARTICLE 7

All are equal before the law and are entitled without any discrimination to equal protection of the law. All are entitled to equal protection against any discrimination in violation of this Declaration and against any incitement to such discrimination.

ARTICLE 8

Everyone has the right to an effective remedy by competent national tribunals for acts violating the fundamental rights granted him by the constitution or by law.

ARTICLE 9

No one shall be subjected to arbitrary arrest, detention or exile.

ARTICLE 10

Everyone is entitled in full equality to a fair and public hearing by an independent and impartial tribunal, in the determination of his rights and obligations and of any criminal charge against him.

ARTICLE 11

Everyone charged with a penal offense has the right to be presumed innocent until proved guilty according to law in a public trial at which he has had all the guarantees necessary for his defense.

ARTICLE 12

No one shall be subjected to arbitrary interference with his privacy, family, home or correspondence, nor to attacks upon his honor and reputation. Everyone has the right to the protection of the law against such interference or attacks.

ARTICLE 13

Everyone has the right to freedom of movement and residence within the borders of each state.

Everyone has the right to leave any country, including his own, and to return to his country.

ARTICLE 14

Everyone has the right to seek and to enjoy in other countries asylum from persecution.

This right may not be invoked in the case of prosecutions genuinely arising from non-political crimes or from acts contrary to the purposes and principles of the United Nations.

ARTICLE 15

Everyone has the right to a nationality.

No one shall be arbitrarily deprived of his nationality nor denied the right to change his nationality.

ARTICLE 16

Men and women of full age, without any limitations due to race, nationality or religion, have the right to marry and to found a family. They are entitled to equal rights as to marriage, during their marriage and at its dissolution.

Marriage shall be entered into only with the free and full consent of the intending spouses.

The family is the natural and fundamental group unit of society and is entitled to the protection of society and the state.

[A disturbing element in this article to some religious observers is whether the provisions apply only to governments or whether nongovernment units, such as churches, can be forced to abide by this rule. This is especially pertinent to religions that look with disfavor on interfaith marriages. Also the Republic of Nauru recently blocked a Nauruan woman's marriage to a Korean on the grounds that such a small number of Nauru natives remain that interracial marriages would soon render them extinct.]

ARTICLE 17

Everyone has the right to own property alone as well as in association with others.

No one shall be arbitrarily deprived of his property.

[This article naturally did not set well with Communist countries where the basic ideology is government ownership of property. Nor did it arouse enthusiasm in underdeveloped countries who have their eye on future expropriation of foreign-owned industry.]

ARTICLE 18

Everyone has the right to freedom of thought, conscience and religion; this includes freedom to change his religion or belief, and freedom, either alone or in community with others and in public or private, to manifest his religion or belief in teaching, practice, worship and observance.

ARTICLE 19

Everyone has the right to freedom of opinion and expression. This right includes freedom to hold opinions without interference and to seek, receive and impart information and ideas through any media and regardless of frontiers.

ARTICLE 20

Everyone has the right to freedom of peaceful assembly and association.

No one may be compelled to belong to any association. [What would such an article do to the international labor movement where union membership is often a prerequisite to holding a job? This is not to say that such requirements are good or bad, but it points out how the idealistic wording of the Universal Declaration is at odds with the practical policies of the world.]

ARTICLE 21

Everyone has the right to take part in the government of his country, directly or through freely chosen representatives.

Everyone has the right of equal access to public service in his country.

The will of the people shall be the basis of the authority of government; this will shall be expressed in periodic and genuine elections which shall be by universal and equal suffrage and shall be held in secret vote or by equivalent free voting procedures.

ARTICLE 22

Everyone, as a member of society, has the right to social security and is entitled to realization, through national effort and international cooperation and in accordance with the organization and resources of each state, of the economic, social and cultural rights indispensable for his dignity and the free development of his personality.

ARTICLE 23

Everyone has the right to work, to free choice of employment, to just and favorable conditions of work and to protection against unemployment.

Everyone, without any discrimination, has the right to equal pay for equal work.

Everyone who works has the right to just and favorable remuneration insuring for himself and his family an existence worthy of human dignity, and supplemented, if necessary, by other means of social protection.

ARTICLE 24

Everyone has the right to form or join trade unions for the protection of his interests.

Everyone has the right to rest and leisure, including reasonable limitation on working hours and periodic holidays with pay.

ARTICLE 25

Everyone has the right to a standard of living adequate for the health and well-being of himself and of his family, including food, clothing, housing and medical care and necessary social services, and the right to security in the event of unemployment, sickness, disability, widowhood, old age or other lack of livelihood in circumstances beyond his control.

Motherhood and childhood are entitled to special care

and assistance. All children, whether born in or out of wedlock, shall enjoy the same social protection.

ARTICLE 26

Everyone has the right to education. . . .

Education . . . shall promote understanding, tolerance and friendships among all nations, racial or religious groups, and shall further the activities of the United Nations for the maintenance of peace.

Parents have a prior right to choose the kind of education that shall be given to their children.

ARTICLE 27

Everyone has the right freely to participate in the cultural life of the community, to enjoy the arts and to share in scientific advancement and its benefits.

Everyone has the right to the protection of the moral and material interests resulting from any scientific, literary or artistic production of which he is the author.

ARTICLE 28

Everyone is entitled to a social and international order in which the rights and freedoms set forth in this Declaration can be fully realized.

ARTICLE 29

Everyone has duties to the community in which alone the free and full development of his personality is possible.

In the exercise of his rights and freedoms, everyone shall be subject only to such limitations as are determined by law solely for the purpose of securing due recognition and respect for the rights and freedoms of others and of meeting the just requirements of morality, public order and the general welfare in a democratic society.

These rights and freedoms may in no case be exercised contrary to the purposes and principles of the United Nations.

ARTICLE 30
Nothing in this Declaration may be interpreted as implying for any state, group or person any right to engage in any activity or to perform any act aimed at the destruction of any of the rights and freedoms set forth herein.

BIBLIOGRAPHY

Acheson, Dean, *Present at the Creation.* New York: Norton, 1969.

Bailey, Sydney D., *The Secretariat of the United Nations.* New York: Praeger, 1964.

Becker, Benjamin A., *Is the United Nations Dead?* Philadelphia: Whitmore, 1969.

Bentwich, Norman, and Martin, Andrew, *A Commentary on the Charter of the United Nations.* London: Routledge & Kegan Paul, 1950.

Donovan, Frank R., *Mr. Roosevelt's Four Freedoms.* New York: Dodd Mead, 1966.

Edmonds, I.G., *Revolts and Revolutions.* New York: Hawthorn, 1969.

Edmonds, I.G., *Taiwan: The Other China.* New York: Bobbs-Merrill, 1971.

Gordenker, Leon, *The UN Secretary-General.* New York: Columbia University Press, 1967.

Group Report, *China and the United Nations.* New York: Manhattan Publishing Company, 1950.

Hammarskjöld, Dag, *Servant of Peace.* Edited by Wilder Foote. New York: Harper's, no date.

Harley, J. Eugene, *Documentary Textbook on the United Nations.* Los Angeles: Center of International Understanding, 1950.

Kelen, Emery, *Hammarskjöld.* New York: Putnam, 1966.

Lash, Joseph P., *Dag Hammarskjöld.* Garden City, N.Y.: Doubleday.

Lie, Trygve, *In the Cause of Peace*. New York: Macmillan, 1954.

Meigs, Cornelia, *The Great Design*. Boston: Little, Brown, 1964.

United Nations, *Everyman's United Nations*. New York, United Nations, 1963.

Vincent, Jack E., *Handbook of the United Nations*. Woodbury, N.Y.: Barron's, 1969.

Von Horn, Carl, *Soldiering for Peace*. New York: McKay, 1967.

PERIODICALS:

New York Times
United Nations World
China News
Time Magazine
Newsweek

Index